THE PUPPET BOOK

the Puppet Book

Bill Hawes

BETA BOOKS • SAN DIEGO

THE PUPPET BOOK

Copyright © 1977 by Bill Hawes.
Beta Books, 10857 Valiente Court
San Diego, California 92124

Library of Congress Cataloging in Publication Data

Hawes, Bill, 1931—
    The puppet book

1.   Puppets and puppet-plays.   I.   Title.
PN1972.H36   791.5'3   77-1992
ISBN 0-89293-034-9

DEDICATION
Dedicated to the creative staff of Puppet Productions, Inc., and to all puppeteers who have helped make puppetry the communications tool that it is today

Table Of
Contents

Preface

As a young lad in elementary school, one of my favorite "cop-out" quotes was "Why does learning have to be such a bore?" I said the same thing about Sunday school. I think about my school years of the past and compare them with my children's experiences in public school today and yes, Sunday school, and realize that things haven't changed too much. Many teachers trained and untrained, with and without teaching certificates, have not learned the rudiments of teaching. Teachers must effectively learn to communicate; unless they do, they cannot be successful. Many professional teachers have forgotten the most important factor in teaching, which is: you must *have* and *keep* the attention of your pupils. Teachers should continually work at this, otherwise the pupils are not listening, they're not involved, and thus they are not motivated to learn. Ten years ago I began to realize that a puppet presentation could be one way in which a teacher could capture the attention of her pupils — and then keep it for a longer period of time. Before realizing it, the pupils are not only listening, they have become involved. If the puppet presentation is properly written and performed, the pupils have indeed experienced learning in a happy, pleasant environment.

I hope this book will motivate you to consider how puppet presentations can help you become a more effective teacher, regardless of the purpose or message. Using puppets as teachers can help you to create a happy learning environment and even make learning fun.

I am deeply grateful to many people for helping me put this book together. First of all to Puppet Production's chief writer and Director of Public Relations, Don Coley, I express my gratitude. Don is the one who so ably took my manuscripts and all my previously printed material, his knowledge of puppetry acquired in the past several months, and wrote this book with style and finesse. To Ollie Coffman, illustrator; Gary Avery, photographer; Dr. Betty Higgins, Educational Consultant; Pat Platt, of The Puppet Playhouse, San Diego; Rev. Robert Kleinschmidt, pastor, First Baptist Church, Lemon Grove, Calif.; and to the staff of Puppet Productions, San Diego, Ca.: Mike Hawes, Fred Catalano, Jeff Fitzwater, Robin Nelson, Walter Smith, and our typists, I say thanks for your many hours of hard, diligent work. Also to my wife, Naomi, who through the years has assisted me in so many ways in making puppetry our life's work.

Bill Hawes

Introduction

The Papago Indian Reservation in southwestern Arizona may seem an unlikely place for a rebirth of interest in puppets and puppetry. But it was there, during a sweltering Easter vacation week in 1970, that a group of San Diego teenagers learned the value of puppets for entertaining, relating, and instruction.

America was troubled by social unrest and racial turmoil in 1970 and the Pago Reservation was no exception. The 100 young people who were on a church missionary trip were greeted with skepticism and apathy when they arrived. But it seemed that their effort, and the special touch of puppets, created a chemistry which broke down sterotypes and cultural barriers. Soon, Anglo teenagers from middle class America were freely sharing with native Americans far removed from their economic circumstances. The use of puppets proved an invaluable tool.

This was not an isolated instance of the utility of puppets. In the intervening years since 1970, literally thousands of puppeteers have re-enacted the spirit of the Papago encounter in differing circumstances. Georgia teenagers have traveled into Central America with their puppet ambassadors, training puppet teams composed entirely of natives and leaving professional puppets with them to enhance their ability to communicate. Other trained puppeteers have done the same in twenty-five foreign countries.

From a modest beginning in the Arizona desert, organized puppetry has experienced dramatic gains. The original church teenagers who formed that first puppet group were also members of a small auditioned singing group which utilized the benefits of puppets during their performances. Known first as The Californians, and later as New Californians II, this group traveled extensively across the United States and Europe, popularizing the use of puppets at every tour stop. Their ability was recognized by a television network when they were selected to perform regularly on a nationwide summer television series.

Subsequent tours emphasized the use of puppets. Because many performances were held in churches, church education leaders first recognized the potential benefits of incorporating the entertaining puppet teachers into their educational programs. The New Californians began conducting training seminars, instructing thousands of adults and teenagers in the fine art of puppetry. For the first time, puppets became involved in a systematic program of instruction at the same time they were entertaining.

Three years after the first use of puppets with the Papago Indians, Puppet Productions, Inc., was founded in response to the tremendous demand generated by the New Californians II training seminars. The success of Puppet Productions, Inc., has been astounding.

More than 35,000 people in all 50 states have been trained in seminars conducted by its professional puppeteers. People who previously would watch puppet performances only for the entertainment value suddenly became aware that they were capable of utilizing this tremendous tool for instruction in their own circumstances. Puppet Productions succeeded in dispelling the myth that puppetry — like magic — was the exclusive domain of a privileged few. The result? Churches, the first to recognize puppets as an instructional vehicle, now have more than 6,000 active puppet teams. These teams do not perform just in religious settings. They have responded to invitations from civic groups, service clubs, PTA, television stations and many more. And their professional performances in secular settings have generated interest in puppetry from additional sources.

Public schools, which have traditionally seen puppets in the domain of crafts rather than instruction, have begun to incorporate the advantages of instructional puppetry into their programs. Pilot programs developed by Puppet Productions have been overwhelmingly accepted and are broadening in scope.

Puppet Productions, Inc., has expanded rapidly since the modest beginnings of its predecessors in 1970. It has presented the puppet as a legitimate instructional tool and trained those interested in puppetry in the professional techniques involved. THE PUPPET BOOK represents the experiences of Puppet Productions as it has popularized puppetry since 1970. Hundreds of thousands of miles, thousands of seminars, and uncounted questions from those eager to learn from a part of the background represented in the following pages. The value of this experience cannot be calculated in dollars. It represents the work and dedication of puppeteers who began, as many readers of this book will begin, with little or no experience or knowledge of puppetry. But they learned through their experiences and their experiences are recorded in THE PUPPET BOOK so that you, in turn, may learn the value and rewards of using puppets as teachers. Good puppetry is not magic, anymore than are good music or athletic performances. It is the result of sound instruction and hard work. The information contained in THE PUPPET BOOK will provide the reader with all the sound instruction necessary. If the reader provides the hard work, he will be able to witness the birth of a personality from lifeless pieces of foam and fabric.

The following pages contain chapters which tell not only about the mechanical operation of puppets, but also give a philosophy and program for the use of puppets in several different settings. THE PUPPET BOOK provides much of what you will need to successfully become a good puppeteer; only one important thing is missing: your imagination. Even as instructional tools, puppets remain highly entertaining characters. They should not be restricted by a lack of puppeteer creativity. So crank up your mind, learn well, and enter the fascinating world of puppets.

1

Why Do Puppets Work?

If puppetry isn't magic, how then does it work? Why are puppets so effective in creating an atmosphere for learning? How can lifeless pieces of foam and material capture the attention of people regardless of age?

The answer is multi-faceted. Many dimensions of the successful chemistry of puppetry can be seen in the experience of displaying professional-quality hand puppets at various education and church conventions. In the hands of a skilled puppeteer, puppets assume life-like qualities. This puppet personality attracts a great deal of attention by those present. Observers of this scene will notice that the puppet generally gains the attention of its audience immediately. He will also note that the audience is actively enjoying the entertainment value of the performance. A very important but intangible factor is the involvement of the audience with the puppet itself. The spectator finds himself caught up in the performance and often identifies in some fashion with the puppet characters; this suggests the closeness of the elements of fantasy and identification. And despite the element of fantasy which is present in puppet shows, *these characters must be believable.*

These factors are considered individually to more fully explain the unique chemistry of puppets.

ATTENTION — The ability of puppets to gain the full and undivided attention of an audience is perhaps the greatest reason why puppets are so successful in relating instructional or purely entertaining material. The other factors mentioned above would be impossible to attain if the puppets did not have the audience's attention. At the same time, elements such as entertainment, fantasy, and involvement all contribute to the ability of the puppet to gain and maintain undivided attention.

Children enjoy learning when the lessons are presented in an entertaining way. Puppets gain their undivided attention.

Novelty is certainly one element in this ability. Quality puppet performances are not commonplace occurances and this variation from everyday experience is a decided advantage for the puppet. The American public has been oversaturated with media campaigns of all descriptions. Students are thoroughly familiar with the typical teacher-student interaction which generally defines contemporary education. We have become a culture which knows what to expect next; we are often familiar to the point of immunity.

But we are not familiar with puppets. We are not acquainted with their abilities and personalities. And because they are different, we notice them. We attend to them in a way in which we are not accustomed. We are immediately ready to listen to what they say. And because we listen more carefully to what they say, we are more open for learning to take place.

This does not mean, however, once the novelty of puppets wears off, that they will no longer serve as useful teachers; because the reasons listed above explain only why the audience initially pays attention to the puppets. The uniqueness of puppets lies in the fact that they have additional abilities which allow them to maintain a refreshing "newness" even after they have been seen hundreds of times.

Convention registrants will venture back to the puppet displays each day the exhibit is open. They return to be entertained, to enjoy themselves. For puppets, worked by experienced and capable puppeteers, are among the most entertaining characters in the world today. Later chapters will more fully develop the ability of puppets to provide entertainment but brief treatment can be provided here. Comedy, drama, musical numbers, pantomine — all are included in the repertoire of puppets, and the entertainment aspect of puppet performances is capable of being individually tailored to the specific audience. Parody and nature are two particularly effective humorous uses for puppets and there is never any want of material for scripts. Famous persons, news events, television programs, and many more sources are available for script material. Using material with which the audience is vaguely familiar, but which is presented in a new and different format, allows the puppets added believability as they imitate their more famous human personalities.

FANTASY is also a big factor in the ability of puppets to successfully relate to their audiences. The motion picture industry tapped this formula in the numerous disaster pictures of the early and mid 70's. Puppets allow a healthier fantasizing in a humorous vein. Not only does the audience identify with a particular puppet or puppets, and become involved in the performance, but they also relate to the unseen puppeteer back stage. The ability of the puppeteer to turn a lifeless dummy into an entertaining personality is an ability which is almost universally envied. Watching someone else create a new life through puppetry is like watching another person sit down to your favorite dessert: you feel a tremendous urge to join in. And so the captivating personality on stage, with its clever quirks and mannerisms, soon becomes manipulated not by the real puppeteer, but by the spectator. "I can do that," is the thought, and there is vicarious enjoyment from performer to audience. Convention participants invariably want to "hold" the puppets and make them work. And, for a few brief moments, they leave the particular realities of their world as they "play" with their puppets. The attraction of the puppet is graphically illustrated, and few people exist who can resist their magnetism.

This fantasizing and identification with both puppet and puppeteer is an excellent example of the active involvement which exists for the spectator during a puppet performance. Many people spend literally thousands of hours in front of their television sets with little or no involvement whatever. You can watch television while eating, conversing, or reading the evening paper. You cannot do these things during a puppet show because the show *commands* your attention. You become involved. And it is in this environment of total attention that quality learning can best occur.

Another factor which must be present in quality puppet productions is the element of REALITY. The puppet play, while enabling the audience to fantasize, must contain a spark of believability. The puppet must be seen as more than the sum of its inanimate parts. It must present a character or personality which is believable. A good example of this is the success of the Sesame Street characters such as Bert and Ernie. Although their conversations are highly humorous and entertaining, they often reflect incidents which are familiar to the lives of most people. If puppet shows were nothing more than cute nonsense, they would not be effective vehicles of instruction because they would lack this important link in maintaining audience attention; believability *is* important.

Puppets are also useful in other areas of learning besides formal instruction. For individuals with learning or emotional difficulties, puppets can sometimes be used as excellent therapeutic tools. Watching the reactions of people to puppets is always an interesting experience: they become actively involved in the performance. But one puppet activity can create opposite reactions in individual members of the audience. If the puppet suddenly turns and starts to converse with a

Puppets are useful to help teachers explain visual presentations. This puppet assists in a geography lesson utilizing a relief map.

particular person, their response will be one of two: either they will shy away in embarrassment, or they will eagerly enter into conversation.

Why these responses? The first person becomes self-conscious at being so involved in the puppet show that the puppet would notice and turn to him. The individual, then, is not fully aware if this involvement is "adult," as seen by himself and his peers, and because of this uncertainty he retreats into a more detached position. It is not unlike a father getting "caught" playing with his son's new electric train. The second individual is not threatened by dialog with a puppet. On the contrary, the situation is completely relaxed and open, and candid comments may result. It is this second individual who reflects the use of puppets as a theatrical tool. Because the circumstances are completely non-threatening for these individuals, they can speak through puppets without feeling inadequacies which they may have placed upon themselves. Psychologists and psychiatrists use the technique of psychodrama to create a non-threatening environment in which individuals can relate without fear; providing these persons with puppets may produce the same result. Although the person provides the voice, it is the puppet in a very real sense who is speaking.

Stuttering is a case in point. This speech impediment is sometimes related to poor self image or an inferiority complex. A person who stutters for this reason may be able to speak perfectly if he is speaking for or through a puppet. Because the puppet becomes the visible personality, and because the puppet has no personality conflicts, there is no reason to feel threatened when speaking for the puppet.

Persons speaking through puppets may also tend to assert themselves more than if they were speaking for themselves. And individuals listening to puppets may

The puppet in this picture is engaged in a conversation with the classroom teacher. Such talks can present useful information to the class in a unique way.

also tend to accept more from a puppet than they would from another human being, even though they realize that a human is, in fact, speaking. These responses to puppets are all possible because puppets are not as frightening as people. And because they don't threaten, it is often much easier for puppets to achieve an atmosphere conducive for quality education and therapy.

Why do puppets work? In the final analysis, it is probably an intangible blend of all of these things. Certainly their novelty is greatly responsible for initially gaining the attention of an audience. From this point, it is up to the puppet to establish its character with the audience. They turn the charm, they entertain, they are lovable; and, puppets are fun.

But there is another reason why puppets work, and it is the most important reason. Puppets are only as successful as the puppeteer. Professional puppetry requires hard work by the puppet team. In this regard, puppetry is no different than any other field of human endeavor. The time-tested formula of hard work equaling success holds true. The grace of the ballerina or Olympic gymnast was not achieved overnight. Professional athletes dedicate themselves to long hours in the solace of the practice field in order to excell before millions of spectators in the real competition. Similarly, the puppeteer must diligently apply himself in rehearsals if his performance is to be judged acceptable. There is no immediate reward for repeatedly practicing the mechanics and fundamentals of puppetry. But the puppeteer who truly desires to give the best possible puppet show will find much satisfaction in the audience response at actual performances.

Yet mastering the techniques of puppetry is not enough. The puppeteer must involve himself in his work. He must be able to create his own personality, or new ones, inside the foam body of his puppet. And that is where the fun begins. The secret world of Walter Mitty can come alive in anyone when they put on their puppet and start performing. This is a necessity! The puppeteer must develop a special relationship with the puppet that results in the puppet appearing to be a natural, expressive, loveable personality. And when this happens puppets work.

Attention, involvement, entertainment, believability, fantasy: all contribute to the successful technique involved in professional quality puppetry. Coupled with a creative puppeteer who brings the puppet to life in stimulating and entertaining fashion, these qualities form the chemistry which makes puppets work.

Sound complicated? It isn't really. Anyone can do it with practice. So keep reading, learning and practicing what you learn. And come further into the puppet world.

2

A Description Of Puppets

The word puppet means different things to different people. This is because the term encompasses several different objects, all of which are called puppets. Few people, for example, are aware that the first puppets were actually shadows.

Shadow puppets, although not popular in this country at the present time, are believed to be the oldest form of puppetry with their early beginnings in China. The exact age of this art is unknown. In shadow puppetry, the stage is darkened except for one light source which serves to cast shadows on a screen. Obviously, these primitive beginnings had several limitations for performing when contrasted to today's methods.

With the shifting of cultural centers to the Greek and Roman Empires, reference is also found to puppets as part of the performing arts. The existence of marionettes as early as 300 B.C. is indicated in remarks

The ostrich marionette is covered with a fabric skin to give it a more life-like appearance.

by Horace. He speaks of one who moves like a wooden puppet pulled by wires. Of course, marionettes are still quite popular today and represent the only form of puppetry for many serious puppeteers. Unlike hand puppets, marionettes are manipulated from above the stage through the use of guide wires connected to the various body parts.[1] The full body of a marionette allows it to actually walk during the performance instead of making the audience imagine that the puppet is walking on its own legs, as is the case with hand-held puppets.

Pat Platt, a professional puppeteer prepares her marionette for a performance in San Diego. In the background is a stage designed for marionette performances.

Marionettes, wooden puppets manipulated by strings or cords, were among the earliest form of puppets.

This poodle and mouse were early prototype of hand puppets created for Puppet Productions, Inc., by Ralph Chesse, of San Francisco.

The ancestors of the present-day hand-held puppet were the glove puppets. These were an extremely popular form of puppet and variations of this form are still found today. Many schools have the students construct sock puppets in craft activities; this is an outgrowth of the basic glove puppet. However, in its endeavor to give evermore natural and realistic performances, puppetry has become quite sophisticated. In so doing, the glove puppet has given way to the lifesized hand puppet. The popularity of this type of puppet in schools and churches has increased dramatically since its introduction.

Herbie is a rod-arm puppet. The arms are manipulated by metal rods and this gives the puppet a more believable quality.

The hand-held puppet presently appears in distinct styles: the rod puppet, the rod-arm puppet, and the human hand and arm puppet.[2][3] In operation, the heads and mouths of these puppets are identical. (See chapter 4.) The basic difference is in the method of manipulating the arms. The rod-arm puppet has smaller, stuffed arms, onto which a metal rod is attached. The rod itself is approximately 24 inches long with a small loop at the end. A vinyl wristlet is attached to the arm of the puppet, just above the hand. This wristlet has a small opening through which the metal rod extends, and it is secured by re-closing the loop. With both rods securely attached to the arms, the puppeteer manipulates the arms of the puppet simply by moving the rods for whatever gestures are desired.

The human hand and arm puppet does not utilize rods. Instead, the puppeteer actually inserts his arm and hand into the puppet and his arm and hand become the arm and hand of the puppet. Gloves the color of the puppet's skin are used to create the correct color for the hands. This puppet is a tremendous addition to the art of puppetry; it allows gestures and manipulations which significantly affect the realism of the puppet production.

Human hand and arm puppets, and rod-arm puppets, have been pioneered and popularized by the work of Puppet Productions, Inc., of San Diego, California. As the leading manufacturer of these puppets, and the leader also in training the general public in the correct use of them, Puppet Productions has accumulated a vast amount of information concerning their use. THE PUPPET BOOK is written with the hand-held puppet in mind. Although most of the material in THE PUPPET BOOK is universal, chapters dealing specifically with manipulations are intended for puppeteers who are interested in using hand-held

Human hand and arm puppets are the most realistic because the puppeteer inserts his hands and arms into the puppet itself.

puppets. They are much more loveable than shadows, easier to operate than marionettes, and they represent the largest and fastest growing division of puppetry today.

The history of puppetry has generally been a history of entertainment. Only recently have the instructional advantages of puppetry been recognized. THE PUPPET BOOK is a compilation of the experiences of instructional puppeteers as they have discovered the ability of puppets to communicate messages as well as pure entertainment. It has every bit of information on puppetry you will need to become an experienced puppeteer. Only one puppet description is missing: the description of *your* puppet as *you* bring it to life — its temperament, personality, gestures, voices and all the rest. Providing this description is what makes puppetry fun!

----

1 Most marionettes have hard wooden faces and unmoveable mouths, while some have the capability for mouth movement by manipulating another string or wire. Also, some marionettes are covered with fabric to keep them from looking "wooden." The photograph of the ostrich marionette is an example of this fabric-coated puppet.

2 ROD PUPPETS. The rod puppet gets its name from a wooden dowling or rod that is fastened securely to the bottom of the head through the neck. The puppeteer grasps the rod with his hand, which is inside the body of the puppet. He is able to manipulate the head up, down and sideways. In more sophisticated rod puppets, the mouth can be opened when the puppeteer pulls down on a string cord with his forefinger. These rod puppets are usually made individually by professional puppeteers. They are made of wood, styrofoam, and paper or plastic maché.

3 ROD ARM AND HUMAN HAND AND ARM PUPPETS. These puppets are generally constructed out of polyfoam and are covered with fabric.

3

The Puppet Director

In athletics, planning for success begins long before the start of actual competition. Coaches map strategy and organize how they expect to accomplish their goals. Similarly, successful businessmen extensively research a project and carefully plan each component in order to ensure operating efficiency. Puppetry is no different.

Good direction is essential for professional quality puppetry. And the central person involved, obviously, is the director. Puppetry is more than one individual with his puppet; to perform quality puppet productions, it is necessary for a team of people to work together just as in most other forms of entertainment. The director must provide the proper amount of guidance to ensure that the puppet team works well together. This is not always an easy task.

The director is combination manager, teacher, promoter, drill sergeant, mother, coach, administrator, psychologist, and referee, all wrapped up in a Norman Vincent Peale personality, with the patience of Job and the endurance of a distance runner. Because many people who are attracted to puppetry are teenagers and young adults, the director must be able to work well with this age group. He must be knowledgeable in the art of puppetry and be able either to think creatively or to assemble a group of creative individuals to provide material for performances. The puppet director, being in charge of the entire operation, must be a responsible individual: one who can delegate responsibility, and one who can exercise sound judgment.

Determining the scope of the director's job is easier if an examination is made of the various functions which must be accomplished by the director. Central to these duties is the scheduling of rehearsal time. Rehearsals must be well-planned and executed if they are to

Rehearsals require an active Director, criticizing the performance and communicating with team members. Here, the Director addresses puppeteers who have watched a dress rehearsal of "Alcohol on Trial."

accomplish their purpose of preparing puppeteers to perform high-quality puppet production. The ability of a puppet team to perform well in puppet shows is directly related to the effort applied during rehearsals. Athletic teams often stress the basics or fundamentals of their sport during practice sessions. The emphasis on these fundamentals, and the repetition of them until they are well-learned, reflects the non-glamorous side of athletics (or puppetry). But the teams which excel in the basics are those which perform well when "the chips are down."

Similarly, rehearsals for puppet performers involve more than simply playing with a puppet. Many dull and routine exercises are also necessary. The director has the responsibility to see that the rehearsal sessions contain all the necessary components for success. The following example of a rehearsal session has proven successful and may serve as a guide for those interested either in starting a new puppet group or improving their present one.

1. Prior to the start of the actual rehearsal, all of the required puppets, stages, sound equipment, and other accessories must be in place. This saves valuable time once the rehearsal itself is started. The director may delegate this job, but he must see that it is accomplished.

2. Rehearsals should start promptly at the scheduled time. Groups such as choirs, PTAs, clubs, etc., frequently meet on a more casual basis and often do not follow a strict schedule. Puppet teams cannot afford this luxury. Each minute represents valuable time which needs to be spent either in individual or team practice. Insisting that puppeteers be prompt establishes an attitude of discipline which carries over to other areas of the rehearsal and is very useful.

3.   Rehearsals should begin with a discussion of coming performances. This discussion should include dates, times, locations, extra rehearsals (if necessary), and tentative plans for the type of show and content. Lists with this information should be printed and distributed to team members well in advance of scheduled dates so that needless conflicts can be avoided. Discussing these items briefly at the beginning of rehearsals insures that all members are kept well-informed, a significant factor in maintaining high morale.

4.   Following discussion of scheduling information, assignments should be made for each member. It is imperative that every individual be aware of his or her part for each performance. These assignments are the responsibility of the director, and he must exercise judgment and diplomacy in this area. As a general rule, assignments should be made which allow every individual to become involved in various role responsibilities. If all team members are approximately equal in ability, parts should reflect this equality by allowing each person to be the "star" occasionally. The director must not, however, assign an inexperienced or un-qualified puppeteer to a role which is too difficult. This is not good for either the puppeteer or puppet team and is reflected in a poor perform-ance. The director should use rehearsals to upgrade the quality of these puppeteers until they are capable of handling more involved parts without difficulty.

5.   Rehearsal should begin for the next scheduled performance. Puppeteers should take their places backstage and fasten copies of the script to the stage in front of them. This helps the puppeteer

follow the tape if the show is pre-recorded. The tape should be played as the puppeteers practice just the lip synchronization (hereinafter referred to as lip sync). They should know both the tape and script well enough to keep the puppet's mouth in close synchronization with the dialog. This is very important! They must be able to lip sync well, especially on the first syllable of the first word of each sentence. The director should observe this from the audience perspective. Listening to the tape and practicing lip sync should be repeated until the director is satisfied that all puppeteers are prepared for the puppet show.

6. After good lip sync has been attained, listen to the tape again, this time practicing the necessary entrances and exits. These are important transitions in a puppet show and must be done well.

7. Play the tape once again, this time emphasizing the personality of the puppet and its movements. Rehearse all hand gestures, head movements, and related activities which make the puppet come alive. The director should make sure that these movements and mannerisms are consistent with the character part and dialog. For the best audience reaction, puppets must perform smoothly and appear natural on stage, and items 5-7 of this rehearsal schedule are designed to achieve this objective

For the inexperienced, it may appear unnecessary to devote exclusive attention to lip sync, entrances and exits, or movement. But such is not the case. Restricting the attention of the puppeteer to just one aspect of his performance will facilitate the mastering of the puppet show and result in a higher quality show. Attempting to master all three techniques at once is confusing and a very inefficient method of rehearsal.

8. If time permits, the preceeding three steps should be repeated in preparation for future performances. This will serve to familiarze the puppeteer with the material of future programs. The director need not insist on perfection at this time, but should not relax the discipline necessary for high rehearsal and performance standards.

9. Each minute of rehearsal time is valuable and must be utilized. If the puppet team is large, it should be divided into groups. While one group is working with the director in the above schedule, the other should be listening to tapes or reading scripts in preparation for future performances. This can also be done by puppeteers who need to rest after extended sessions of the rehearsal.

10. Attention must be given to the sequence of numbers in the upcoming puppet show. If there are a variety of musical numbers or skits, the puppeteers must organize their backstage activity to insure a smooth transition of puppets and props from one skit to the next. A common failure of many puppet teams in their inability to progress smoothly from one act to another during a variety show. It is the responsibility of the director to see that there are no embarrassing periods of silence (or panic) between skits. In fulfilling his responsibility the director cannot assume that the transition will proceed smoothly just because the puppeteers are aware of it. Rehearsal is a time for practicing transitions backstage as well as performances on stage. Puppets, tapes, props, and any other items which are necessary for the performance must be organized backstage so the puppeteers can get to them quickly. Adequate direction in this area is essential if professional quality puppet shows are desired.

11. To close the rehearsal, distribute copies of scripts and tapes to new puppeteers present so they can become familiar with the material at home. This will also give them time to practice lip sync, but they should be given basic instruction in this technique before proceeding. Chapter 5 contains instruction in proper lip sync and mouth manipulation.

12. Discourage visitors from attending rehearsal. When non-puppet-team members are present, the efficiency of the rehearsal is drastically reduced. Performing before audiences should be done only when the puppet team is capable of quality performances. Since this is not the case during rehearsal sessions, attendance should be restricted to puppet team members.

This rehearsal schedule contains the essential framework which can be adapted for use by the individual puppet groups. It is recommended that rehearsals contain not only the basics of this framework, but also seek to vary the routine of rehearsal so it does not become routine to the point of boredom. The director should plan some special project occasionally which renews the puppeteer's interest in rehearsals. Remember, the director is not just a technical critic, but is a suggester and motivater as well. The director must be infectiously enthusiastic! Rehearsals which are well-organized, yet reflect the creative flare of the director, are extremely beneficial to the overall effectiveness of the puppet team.

When the director is discovering ways to be innovative within the basic rehearsal framework, he or she is also serving as an excellent example for the puppet team as a whole. The puppeteers, in turn, seek outlets for their creativity, and the net result is the addition of excellent skits, scripts and songs to your puppet team repertoire.

While on the subject of creative expression, there are several activities which the director can initiate which will tap the abilities of his puppeteers. These activities can be used during rehearsal periods where the director and one or two puppeteers may excuse themselves without affecting the rehearsal. The first is designed to enhance the versatility of the group by increasing the number of voices which may be used with the puppet character. This simply involves the director and one puppeteer using a separate room from the rest of the rehearsal. The director then challenges the puppeteer to create various voices (little boy, grandma, Donald Duck, etc.). Initially there is some resistance and a feeling of self-conciousness felt by the puppeteer, but this can be overcome in a secure atmosphere and with a highly supportive director. The director should use this time to encourage the puppeteer to develop as many voices as possible and he should not be discouraged if the puppeteer does not respond immediately. After a brief period of time, however, the puppeteer usually experiences greater freedom, and will begin to practice the voices on his own time. The director who takes the time to work with his puppeteers in this manner will be pleasantly pleased with the results.

Another useful activity involves the director and two puppeteers. (This may also be accomplished by asking the puppeteers to pair up, and the entire puppet team can then work on this exercise at one time.) The director suggests a theme for the puppeteers and they have a brief period of time — usually five minutes — in which to create a skit on the subject. This activity is designed to foster creative thinking, and is very useful in building the puppeteers' ability to perform ad-lib plays. This can also be used as a "brainstorming" session for the creation of new script material with each pair of puppeteers contributing pieces to a creative puppet script.

In addition to the more creative activities which stimulate the development of the puppet team, the director must design activities for rehearsal which build the fundamental skills of the puppeteers. One excellent activity used to develop puppeteer ability is to seat the puppet team in a circle, without their puppets. The entire group then counts to 100, keeping lip sync with their hands. This exercise allows everyone to view the techniques of other puppeteers, and allows the puppet team to notice incorrect or sloppy techniques of puppeteers who require additional instruction. Because

A good exercise for puppeteers is practicing techniques of mouth manipulation without puppets. Sitting in a semicircle allows puppeteers to check each other.

most people occasionally get sloppy and develop bad habits, this exercise is beneficial for all puppeteers. It also is an excellent method for new puppeteers to train by example of the more accomplished puppeteers.

The same format may also be used to develop puppet movements. With puppeteers seated in a circle, and with puppets being used, the director can ask the puppeteers to act out a particular emotion, behavior, character trait, etc. Watching others in the puppet team follow out this exercise is particularly beneficial to the puppeteer who can master the techniques of good puppetry but has difficulty being creative.

It needs to be reemphasized here that although these exercises are sometimes fun and humorous, the director must maintain the necessary discipline required for a learning experience. The director must

Practicing manipulation with the puppets is another good technique for the group to do as a unit.

constantly stress the fact that all aspects of the puppet rehearsal are geared toward performing a high quality puppet show. The director must never be placed in the position of babysitting a group of teenagers or of supervising a social activity. Puppet teams which recognize that rehearsals are a necessary means toward an end are successful. Teams which view rehearsals any less seriously will not perform up to their potential capabilities.

The director may also wish to devote some rehearsal time to prop construction (if necessary), costume designing, script writing, sound recording, or other related items which contribute to the success of the puppet team.

It is obvious that the director must be a person who has ample time and energy to devote to his job. Organizing and supervising rehearsals is just part of his job. Additional tasks for which the director is responsible include scheduling, promotion, and recruiting.

Problems related to scheduling are not what might be expected. Puppet teams who strive for excellence are in constant demand because of the highly entertaining nature of their presentations. Puppet directors will be requested to schedule their teams for churches, schools, civic groups, service clubs, and even public service time on some television stations. The director must be extremely careful not to overschedule his team. Puppet teams cannot be overscheduled and maintain excellence. Since the success of one show does not guarantee the success of future shows, adequate rehearsal time must be planned before committing the team to performance dates. It is not easy to say "No" and the director will be pressured into scheduling his team too frequently. But the director must be aware of this danger, and plan accordingly.

When considering scheduling, it is important to understand the benefits of discussing future engagements with the puppet team at the beginning of each rehearsal, as discussed earlier. This allows the puppet team to express itself with regard to the frequency of rehearsal and performance dates. The director who is attentive to the comments of his team will be aware of their feelings and can act to schedule fewer or greater numbers of puppet shows, depending on the wishes of the team members, as well as on production needs.

Recruiting is a significant responsibility of the director. A puppet team which does not get new members often seems to grow inward, to stagnate from the lack of new ideas and fresh blood. It is the responsibility of the puppet director to encourage interested persons to become involved in one of the various aspects of puppetry. The same task, only on a much larger scale, faces the director who is in the process of organizing a new puppet team from scratch. Similar principles are involved in recruiting for either new or existing puppet teams. The following outline may be helpful to follow.

1. The first job involved in recruiting is to make potential team members aware of the opportunity. The director must announce that places on the puppet team are available and he should encourage those interested in auditioning to do so. Experience has shown that young persons below junior high age do not perform well in teams comprised mostly of high school and college-age puppeteers. (Older elementary school students do extremely well in instructional puppetry when performing before other students. This will be discussed later in the chapter "A Puppet Philosophy for Schools.") Therefore, most direc-

tors may wish to restrict auditions to those in 7th grade and above.

2. Auditions should not begin until enough professional quality puppets are available for use. Performing with top quality puppets bring out the best in auditions. Also, the enjoyment of the audience and therefore the success of the puppet play is partially dependent on the quality of puppets used. Even the best puppeteer is restricted in his ability to teach and entertain when using amateur puppets.

3. Auditions must be concerned with several important factors. The interested person must have the time required to become proficient, and be committed to the high standards of excellence which are set by the director. This may be expressed by a willingness to faithfully attend rehearsals and performances. Before the actual work with puppets begins, the candidate should be informed about the performance and discipline standards which are expected of all puppeteers. Many problems can be avoided if this is clarified before the puppeteer joins the team.

4. Each puppeteer must be capable of achieving good lip sync. Not all people can do this, and the director must be sure that the candidate can lip sync before accepting him as a puppeteer. Successful puppet teams, however, are comprised of more than just puppeteers. Extremely creative and talented individuals may be unable to master the basic techniques of puppetry but may, on the other hand, be able to make extremely valuable contributions as puppet team members with other responsibilities. The director should challenge and encourage these individuals to become involved with other essential activities such as script writing,

prop and stage construction, taping for pre-recorded shows, and operating sound and lighting systems. Although individuals who perform these tasks may not receive all the credit that puppeteers receive, they are nevertheless important to the overall success of the puppet team. The director who can enlist capable non-puppeteer members for his puppet team to perform these valuable services, will have accomplished a great deal in guaranteeing the success of his puppet team.

5.   Once the director selects a person to become a puppet team member, that individual takes part in all activities of the team.

Not all of the director's responsibilities are involved in rehearsal and behind-the-scenes activity. He must also take an active role in the actual performance. The director must view performances with a critical eye, constantly looking for things which need to be improved. In addition to the puppet show itself, the director also needs to analyze sound, lights, and other related facts of the production. In this regard, the director is similar to the coach in athletics who reviews the performances of each player after the contest. The director reviews the performance of each puppeteer individually and of the puppet production in general. The natural tendency of the puppeteer, a tendency often reinforced by favorable audience reaction, is to become complacent — satisfied with his performance. The director must see that this does not happen. He must constantly demand more, requiring an excellence from the puppet team which they would not otherwise seek to attain.

The director is a person whose importance cannot be overemphasized. In addition to the duties already mentioned, the director must be capable of doing numerous other things which are involved with working with people. The director will be called upon to mediate disputes of various natures which are the inevitable result of a number of persons working together on the same project. He will need to exercise diplomacy in correcting situations which may arise. He will need to be firm, yet gentle, with his puppet team. There will be times of excitement tempered by discouragement. The director, like a general, will have to rally his troops when the glamour and excitement of initial combat has passed.

This, then, is the puppet director. It is the most important position on the puppet team, and requires an extraordinary individual to fill it.

It is important to correctly position the hand inside the puppet
head. The four fingers should be in the roof of the mouth and the
thumb should be below, in the jaw.

4

Manipulation: The Mouth

The puppet director is the central force in the organization and smooth functioning of the puppet team. But the puppeteer is the central factor in the performance itself. The puppeteer is, after all, the one whose abilities are required to animate the puppet and entertain the audience. Several different functions of the puppeteer will be discussed but the most important is manipulating the mouth properly. Because mouth manipulation is one of the most basic aspects of puppetry, improper manipulation is quickly noticed by the audience and detracts seriously from their enjoyment.

An elementary, yet often over-looked principle of correct mouth manipulation is holding the puppet properly. Many beginning puppeteers are unable to accomplish good lip sync and mouth manipulation because they do not know exactly where their hands

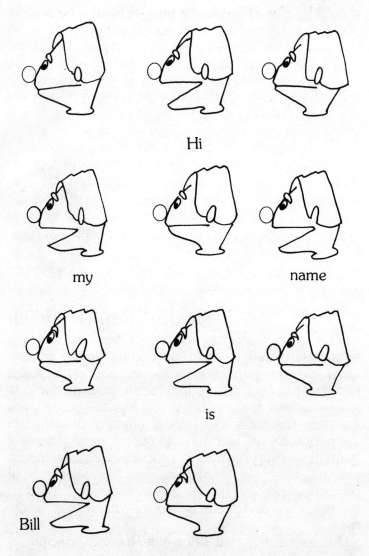

"Hi, my name is Bill." This correctly shows when the mouth should be open for the spoken word. The mouth is originally closed and opens for each word, then remains closed after the conversation ends.

should be placed inside the puppet head. The accompanying drawings help illustrate the correct position for the hand. You will notice from the drawings that *the four fingers should be in the roof of the mouth and the thumb should be below, in the jaw. Both the fingers and the thumb should rest on the cloth-covered mouth, not the foam covering it.* If the hand of the puppeteer is small, it may be necessary to insert a piece of polyfoam in the upper or lower mouth cavities to make a snuggly fitting puppet. Once the puppet has been properly fitted, the puppeteer can begin manipulating it.

Opening and closing a puppet mouth involves the use of arm and hand muscles which are not ordinarily used. This will cause fatigue, even in shorter performances, until the puppeteer gets used to manipulating puppets. Practicing lip sync with the arm straight up will help build these muscles and this practicing should be done with both hands since the good puppeteer must be able to work puppets with either hand.

The key to good mouth manipulation is accurate synchronization of the spoken work and the opening of the mouth. *Particular care should be made to opening the mouth on the first syllable of the first word of each sentence.* This helps create a good impression for the rest of the sentence. Missing the synchronization at this crucial point is clearly noticeable to the audience and dramatically reduces the quality of the show. When opening the mouth, keep in mind that *it is the lower jaw which drops during speech – the upper lip does not go up.* This is a serious weakness in beginning puppeteers. Begin to practice this movement without the puppet so you can make sure your thumb drops while the fingers remain parallel to the ground. This is not a natural tendency and will require a great deal of patience and practice. But that practice will pay off in a puppet which

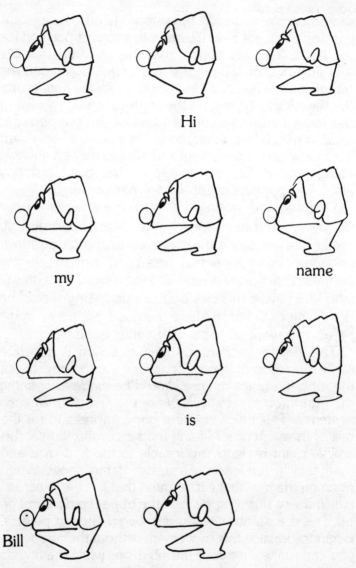

Hi

my

name

is

Bill

"Hi, my name is Bill." Beginning puppeteers frequently make the mistake of biting their words, that is, they begin with the puppet mouth open and close the mouth when the word is said. This is incorrect.

looks natural when it speaks. A good exercise to help
the beginning puppeteer master this technique is
simply to put the hand under a table top or some other
stationary object and repeat the dropped thumb motion. Intersperse this exercise with another where the
puppeteer does not use any stationary objects but has
his hand and arm extended above his head. This is
necessary to more closely simulate actual performance
conditions.

Another commonly mistake made by beginning
puppeteers is biting of words, i.e., closing the mouth
with each word instead of opening it. This tendency
must be watched closely by both puppeteers and
director to insure that only correct manipulation is
performed. Quality puppet teams should never be
troubled by this mistake. Both of these technical points,
the dropped thumb and mouth opening instead of
closing, are important considerations for manipulating
the puppet in a natural manner.

When people talk, they do not open their mouths as
wide as possible for every word. Neither should
puppets. Since the goal of the puppeteer is to create a
"natural" personality in his puppet, the mouth should
be open wide only if the script calls for it, such as yawns,
yells, or exaggerated expressions. This gives the puppet
a special impact when the mouth is opened wide.

Some beginning puppeteers have a tendency to
move their puppets around too much during performances. This detracts from the puppet that is
"speaking" and confuses the audience. Only the
puppet that is actually speaking should be moving its
mouth. While the other puppets need to be responsive
to the speaker, they cannot be so animated in mouth or
body that they take the audience's attention away from
the speaker.

Another aspect related to manipulating the mouth is
maintaining eye contact with the audience. This is

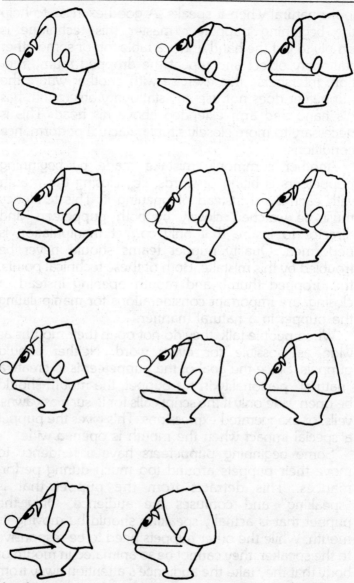

Another mistake of inexperienced puppeteers is moving the head up instead of dropping the jaw. Even if the correct lip sync is used, this presents an unnatural look.

imperative if the puppet that is speaking is going to appear believable to the audience.

Lip sync is the key to quality puppetry, but it involves more than just moving the hand in a particular fashion. It takes practice and familiarity with the script being presented. No puppeteer can lip sync well if he is not acquainted with the script and able to anticipate upcoming words. The tape must be listened to repeatedly to learn both the dialog and the pauses. As an additional help, the puppeteers should have the script directly in front of them during the actual performance. The scripts can be attached to the stage and in this way they serve the same function as cue cards for an actor. But no puppeteer should ever attempt to read the scripts without being thoroughly familiar with the tape itself.

Mouth manipulation *is* lip sync, and lip sync *is* practice. Puppeteers who take pride in their work will accept nothing less than perfection in lip sync for their puppet productions.

5

Manipulation: Rod Arms

The importance of accurate lip sync by the puppeteer cannot be overstressed. But lip sync by itself is not enough to bring the puppet to life. Human speakers have particular mannerisms and make various gestures when speaking. Puppets should be the same way: they should develop arm movements which complement the spoken word and present a more complete personality to the audience. This is possible with the use of rods attached to the puppet arms.

The rods are narrow metal strips, approximately two feet long and the thickness of a clothes hanger. They have a small grip on one end and a loop on the other. The loop end is attached to a vinyl wristlet which goes on the arm of the puppet, just above the wrist, so it is concealed by a long sleeved shirt or blouse. The diagram illustrates how this is done. Once the rods are properly connected, the puppeteer can begin practicing various arm and hand movements.

Beginning puppeteers should manipulate just one rod and allow the other arm to hang down.

Beginning puppeteers should never attempt to operate both arms at the same time; good puppetry comes in stages! With one hand operating the mouth, the second hand should be used to operate one arm until the puppeteer has reached the level of proficiency required to use both arms simultaneously. When using just one arm, let the other arm and rod hang down at the puppet's side, the puppets are manufactured in such a way that the arms hang naturally. The puppeteer can then concentrate on operating the other arm and should strive to develop and perfect as many movements as possible. When this is done, he should practice alternating the arm used in the performance.

Rod arm puppets are capable of a wide range of expressions and gestures as illustrated in these pictures.

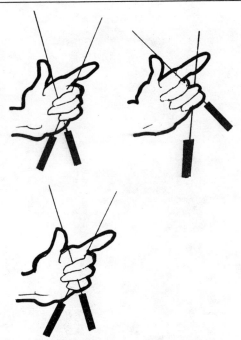

These three drawings illustrate how one hand can be used to hold, and manipulate, both rod arms. Practice and individual preference will determine which method you prefer.

In other words, if the puppeteer used his right hand inside the puppet, his left will be free to operate both rod arms, one at a time. By having the puppet scratch his head with one hand and point with the other, the performance appears more realistic and the audience enjoyment is greater. All the puppeteer needs to do is gently drop one of the rods and pick up the other. Switching from one arm to the other allows both the beginning and experienced puppeteer to give puppets a human-like quality through the use of gestures. As in all phases of puppetry, this maneuver requires practice before the puppeteer becomes comfortable and the transition from one arm to the other is a smooth one.

After the puppeteer has mastered the art of manipulating one rod arm at a time, he may begin practice on working both rod arms with his free hand. This is not as difficult as it might first appear, but must follow the proficient use of one rod at a time. The illustration shows how the two rods should be held in the hand. Notice that the rods are held above the handles and rest in the fingers, not the palm of the hand. Specific movements resulting from manipulating both rods can only be learned by experimentation and practice. One basic gesture which can be done rather easily is that of the puppet clapping his hands, the result of pressing the thumb and index finger together.

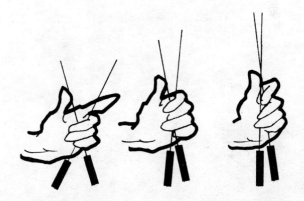

Manipulating both rods with one hand is not as difficult as it might first appear. This illustration shows how a puppet can be made to clap his hands; simply move the thumb and forefinger together and then apart. This brings the puppet's hands together.

Experienced puppeteers can manipulate both rod arms with one hand as seen in this picture from the front.

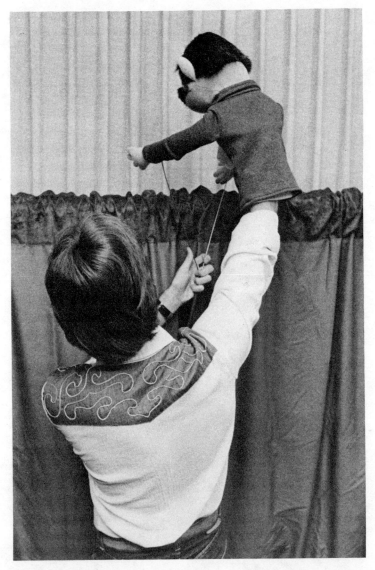

This picture shows a view from backstage of a puppeteer using both rods with one hand.

As the puppeteer becomes proficient in the more basic aspects of puppetry, he will want to experiment, practice. Use your imagination to create added character in your puppets. Proficiency in manipulating rod arms is one of the keys to successful puppetry.

6

Manipulation: Human Hand And Arm

Human hand and arm puppets provide a new dimension in realistic puppetry. These puppets allow the puppeteer to insert his arms into the puppet and provide the opportunities for human movement which do not exist with rod arm puppets. For the most complete operation of the human hand and arm puppet, two puppeteers are necessary. Discussion of human hand and arm puppets will be divided into usage by one and two puppeteers.

SINGLE PUPPETEER. One puppeteer is capable of operating the human hand and arm puppet. He uses one hand to manipulate the puppet and inserts the free arm into the puppet to become the puppet's arm. The puppeteer wears a glove which matches the skin color of the puppet and this glove hand extends out of an especially sewn shirt or blouse. The gloved hand goes through the elasticized sleeve and extends out the non-

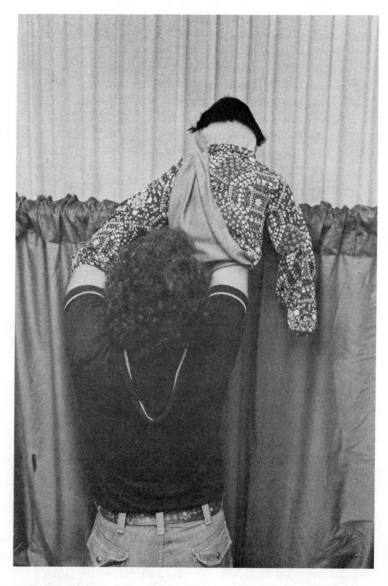

This puppeteer is using a hand and arm puppet by placing one hand in the mouth and the other into one of the puppet arms.

elasticized opening. The elasticized sleeve is then pulled up the puppeteer's arm toward the shoulder. The regular sleeve has two velcro patches which allow the sleeve to be cuffed tightly at the wrist. The foam arm of the puppet is designed to join the puppeteer's forearm and usually rests on or near the puppeteer's elbow. Human hand and arm puppets, like their rod arm counterparts, are designed in such a way that arms not being used or manipulated hang naturally to the side of the puppet.

TWO-MAN PUPPETS. If the use of both arms of a human hand and arm puppet is desired, two puppeteers are required to manipulate the puppet. One puppeteer operates the mouth and the second puppeteer becomes the arms. Experience has shown that the taller of the two puppeteers should operate the head, since the relative heights of the puppeteers will determine how comfortably they will be able to work together. The two puppeteers should position themselves as closely as they can, with the puppeteer operating the head stationed behind the "arm puppeteer." Having the two puppeteers aligned this way is recommended; a reversal of their positions makes operation of the puppet more difficult.

Positioning the "mouth puppeteer" behind his partner is desirable for the two puppeteers to keep the proper body depth, a distance between the hands and body of the puppet. To make the puppet appear natural, the hands must remain approximately 8-10 inches in front of the body. Humans do not usually hold their hands to their chests and neither should puppets. With the arm puppeteer in front of his partner, it is easier to maintain this necessary distance. This position allows the arm puppeteer to look up from under the puppet's body and see exactly what he is doing. This is extremely important when the hands are used to pick

Cooperation is necessary when both arms of a human hand arm puppet is used. One puppeteer manipulates the mouth and the other becomes both arms of the puppet. These pictures show the position of each puppeteer.

up items, scratch the puppet's head, or in other activities where visual coordination is necessary. If the mouth puppeteer is in front, this visual contact is much more difficult. If, for any reason, the positions of the puppeteers must be reversed, it is advisable to have them perform from the standing, rather than the kneeling position. This position allows better eye contact for the rear puppeteer, since it usually gives more room behind the stage in which he can maneuver.

Several important techniques need to be mentioned about using human hand and arm puppets. One of these is the need to coordinate the movements of the arms and head. Both puppeteers should talk to each other behind stage, if a pre-recorded tape is being used. The mouth puppeteer, for example, frequently presses forward until he is too close to the stage, thereby eliminating the necessary body depth of 8-10 inches. Since the arm puppeteer has a better perspective, he will need to tell his partner to move back (slowly, not in one swift jerk) until the proper body depth is reestablished. Cooperation like this is important, and can be obtained with practice and dialog between partners. The puppet director will want to make sure that assignments for two-man human arm and hand puppets are based on the ability of the puppeteers to work well together.

In addition to maintaining the correct body depth of approximately 8-10 inches, the relative height of the hands in relationship to the chest is also important. The hands must be chest high to appear natural. Holding the hands too high or low makes an unnatural and sloppy performance. Hands held too high, for example, hide the face of the puppet and interfere with the audience's viewing the correct lip sync. One method of maintaining the correct height is to rest the hands on

the stage, since the stage level should be approximately the same height as the puppet's chest.

Both the correct body depth and height of the hands are important to maintain throughout the production. This includes entrances and exits. Some puppeteers relax too soon after a performance and do not exit properly. The puppeteers must maintain the conversation and cooperation during the exit or the human hand and arm puppet will look like the head is going in one direction and the hands in another! Do not ruin a quality puppet production with a poorly executed exit. The last impression you make on your audience is an important one. Puppeteers who are just beginning to operate human hand and arm puppets, or partners who have not worked together before, may find it to their advantage to practice in front of a mirror. By observing their reflection, they can gain the perspective of the audience and see if any corrections need be made in the puppet manipulations. This is a good rehearsal technique which allows the puppeteers to critique themselves. The puppet director should critique the actual performances.

It was mentioned earlier that it is desirable to have the taller puppeteer work the head . Some adjustment of heights can be made by having the puppeteers kneel on pads of different thicknesses or sit on short stools. Comfort is a major consideration to be taken into account with human hand and arm puppets. Inevitably the quality of the performance is affected if the puppeteers are not comfortable.

Two puppeteers can work more closely if they kneel with their knees alternating with each other. For example, the "mouth puppeteers" right leg, "arm puppeteers" right leg, "mouth puppeteer's" left leg, "arm puppeteer's" left leg.

These three drawings represent different views the audience can have of a human hand and arm puppet. The first puppet is too high and the sleeve of the puppeteer's arm is seen. The second picture is also incorrect, with the puppet held too low and the hands too high in relationship to the head. The bottom illustration correctly pictures the position of the hands and arms. This gives a natural appearance to the performance.

Human hand and arm puppets allow a variety of arm movements which are not possible with rod arm puppets. The puppeteer will want to experiment with his puppet to see what gestures he can use. There is no limit to the number of combination of gestures for human hand and arm puppets, just as there is no limit to the gestures made by humans. Some basic gestures, however, are listed here for the beginning puppeteer. These actions should be performed as if done by real people. Make your puppets extensions of your own personality. Remember: puppets aren't dummies, they are "real" characters!

Human hand and arm puppets are capable of human-like movements. They can "read" from books, lead singing, or be just plain tired.

Some Basic Gestures For Human Hand And Arm Puppets

"His" (God's) Pointing up with finger or hand.

Personal Noun (I, me, we) Palm to puppet's chest.

"You" Pointing to crowd.

Scared Hands over eyes. Then open up top finger.

Bored Hands on side of face. Hands on stage. Twiddling thumbs.

Prayer Hands folded.

Question (e.g., "Where am I?") Palms up. Hands moving side to side. Head moving.

Personal Question (e.g., "Who's your tailor?") Palm up, hand pointed down to person.

"Ain't that a kick in the head!" Hit head with open palm.

"Boy, is it hot!" Wipe sweat off forehead with two fingers.

Sleeping Head turned to side resting on hand with other hand over eyes, or also supporting head.

Emphasis Loosely closed fist, thumb on top, hand turned up and down.

"Get out!" Pointing finger with sweeping direction toward door. Shake fist.

"For example" Palm up in sweeping gesture.

"No" Palm down in sweeping gesture.

Coughing Hit chest with fist. Cover mouth with fist.

Shock Hands to side of mouth. Mouth open. One hand to chest. Mouth open.

"Then" (Past action) Turn to side. Motion to back of stage with sweeping gesture.

Smile With index finger start at corner of mouth and go up in a smiling fashion.

7

The Puppet Personality

How often have you heard the phrase, "It's so unlike him to do that?" Have you ever stopped to realize why such statements are made? Essentially, they are made because a person says or does something which is inconsistent with the pattern of behavior which, through experience, has become expected of him. People develop personalities, patterns of behavior, by which they are identified. Puppets should do the same.

Puppets need to have their own distinct personalities; they need to develop a consistency of character so their audiences know basically what to expect. It is confusing to audiences, particularly younger ones, to have a puppet character perform in different roles.

An illustration may help make this point. The television program *Sesame Street* uses puppets as characters in its show. Three of these puppet characters

are Bert, Ernie, and Oscar. The personalities of these
three puppet characters have been developed to the
point where viewers of the program know exactly what
to expect in the way of behavior. Oscar, for example, is
a grouch. He lives in a trash can and the thought of
something clean or happy is an irritation to him. He
speaks with a gruff voice. These factors make up Oscar
(at least superficially). Having developed Oscar's identity in the minds of viewers of *Sesame Street,* it is
inconceivable that he would suddenly appear on some
future program dressed neatly in a suit, speaking softly
in a high-pitched voice and living in a mansion.
Professional puppeteers would never make this mistake, but inexperienced ones often do. They have the
same puppet operated by several different puppeteers,
with countless voices, and playing widely divergent
parts. Puppets are not like movie actors that can play
the good guy in one movie and the bad guy in the next.
They must develop a particular personality and consistently relate this personality to the audience. When
this happens, the audience begins to relate to the
puppet character, and learning is better able to occur.

Several factors are involved in developing and
maintaining a consistent personality. Basic to an understanding of these factors is the realization that each
puppet is unique; each is an individual. During the
cutting of head and body, the sewing of the fabric
"skins," and the gluing of wigs, noses, and eyes, the
puppet gains an identity greater than its inanimate
parts. Somewhere in the manufacturing process from
the bolt to the box, the puppet becomes a personality —
and the good puppeteer will exploit this to full advantage.

One important aspect of the personality, often
overlooked, is the individual mannerisms of the
puppeteer. Each puppeteer has a particular style which

is different from that of other puppeteers and this style is reflected in the operation of the puppet. Ideally, the same puppeteer will always operate the same puppet character so the character develops a consistent style and identity with the audience. Head movements, arm gestures, mannerisms, lip sync techniques; all these functions need to remain essentially the same as the puppet develops its identity with the audience.

A second function of personality is that of the voice. Inexperienced puppeteers and puppet teams often think nothing of using three or four voices for one puppet. This should not be done. A determination about voice should be made when the puppet personality is being developed; once a puppeteer or other person has been selected to speak for the puppet, the role should be made permanent. It is sometimes amusing to watch voice tracks dubbed into performances of well-known performers — it is novel — but only because the real voice is firmly established in the minds of the audience. Do not allow your puppets to have different voices speaking for them. It only makes the puppet's job of relating to the audience that much more difficult. Related to this function of personality is the puppet's vocabulary. If a puppet character is being developed to represent a college professor, the vocabulary of his scripts should be more extensive than that of an uneducated laborer puppet. This is a subtle point, but one which good puppet teams will want to follow.

Attitudes and behavior represent another facet of personality. Is the character always in a good mood? Or bad? Does the behavior of the character reflect kindness and sensitivity? Or is the puppet character centered around his own ego? Puppet teams will need to pay particular attention to this — maintaining a consistent portrayal of the puppet.

At this point, it may be necessary to mention that this consistent representation of a particular character with a specific puppet *is* possible to achieve without unnecessarily restricting the puppet to playing just one role. With slight changes, one puppet can be made to play additional characters without confusing the identities involved. This can be done by making slight modifications of costumes, hair style, hair color, facial hair, etc., coupled with a change in puppeteer, voice, or attitudes and behavior. The important consideration here is that each character be consistently used. An Anglo man puppet, for example, could have the personality of an elementary school principal when it is used with a receding blond wig, suit coat and tie. The same puppet, with full black wig, moustache, colorful shirt and beads, could take on the personality of a hippie. In addition to the visual changes made in this example, voices and perhaps puppeteers will also need to be changed. This allows a single puppet to play more than one role without compromising the identity of either one. Other visual or voice changes could be used to create even more characters, if necessary.

The professional quality hand puppets pictured in this book and manufactured by Puppet Productions are available with detachable hair, wigs, and moustaches so that one puppet has the versatility of playing more than a single role.

Thus far, instructions have been given on how puppets assume and maintain a personality all their own. The importance of following these guidelines cannot be over-emphasized. And there are additional rules which, if not followed, will destroy the puppet character in the eyes of the audience. Remember that the puppeteer, in scripts, mannerisms, lip sync, etc., strives to create the impression that the puppet is a genuine character. The goal is to have the audience relate to the puppet as a personality. With this in mind, there are several cardinal rules which must be followed in order to preserve this impression.

1. Puppets should represent personalities. In the hands of a skilled puppeteer, they represent more than foam and fabric. They should be seen — by the audience only during actual performances, when they are "alive." For this reason, never refer to the puppets as puppets in front of the audience. This conflicts with the desire to make them more than puppets. Either call the puppets by name or refer to them as "friends" or some other similar terms.

2. Never allow the audience (especially small children) to see the puppets before or after a show. The puppets should be concealed from view before or after performances to help preserve their personalities. Inquisitive children will invariably rush up to the stage after the show so they can see the puppets. For this reason, the puppets should be packed as soon as possible. If the children ask where the puppets went answer them with something similar to, "Our friends have already gone; they will be back another time."

3. Although everyone deserves recognition for accomplishments, it is better not to introduce the puppeteers. The audience should be left with the impression that the puppets were the actual performers, not the puppeteers. If introductions are felt necessary or desired, printing the names on a program is the best method. Announcing the names will also suffice. NEVER introduce puppeteers as "Fred who worked Ralph, Lisa who worked George," etc. The identities of the puppets and puppeteers must not overlap in the minds of

the audience. The personality of the puppet must stand by itself.

The puppet personality is a critical factor in the success of the puppet production. It is through these personalities that the audience will relate to the production and what is being said. Often, the ability of the audience to identify a particular personality characteristic will allow learning to occur without regard to what is being said. A viewer can see in the selfish personality of a puppet traits similar to his own — and resolve to change them. Such an impact is possible from the development of the puppet personality alone. The puppet team will need to develop a group of puppets with widely divergent character traits to allow maximum flexibility in programming.

For some, the development of a new personality within a puppet is not an easy thing. Others excel at it. But it is certain that all puppeteers must accomplish this at least to a minimum extent if they are to be successful. This is one of the truly "fun" parts of puppetry. Although it will require practice to perfect the personality, the dull routine of rehearsals is not an active factor. The development of the personality lies in the creative reaches of the mind; in the imagination of the puppeteer. At first it may not be easy — you may feel somewhat inhibited. But as you develop this particular skill, you will find it to be one of the most satisfying in puppetry.

8

Staging

An area which is closely related to the puppet personality is the action of the puppet while on stage. Puppeteers should develop the individual personality of each puppet as they establish its identity, but there are some common factors which should be utilized with all puppets on stage.

One of the first considerations in staging is getting the puppets on and off stage. Because most stages used with hand-held puppets do not have curtains, the puppets must arrive on stage in full view of the audience. These entrances should be as natural as possible. The easiest entrance is to have the puppet appear as if he were walking up a flight of stairs. The puppet does not suddenly appear, but arrives gradually, one step at a time. This action requires the puppeteer to keep his forearm straight up, moving slightly forward as he "bounces" the puppet onto the stage. With each

The puppet entrance is very important. The puppet should appear to bounce up into the stage as if it were walking up stairs. With each bounce, the puppet comes more fully into the audience's view. Notice the head itself remains horizontal, with eyes looking straight ahead.

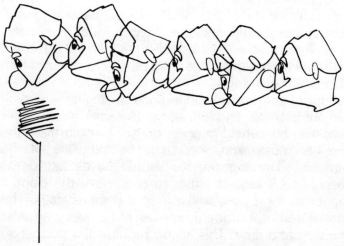

This illustration shows the puppet bouncing up but the head "nods" up and down. This should not be done.

bounce of the arm, the puppet comes more fully into view. When the puppet leaves the stage, this process is reversed. The puppet must not vanish suddenly, but naturally disappear as if descending stairs. Each bounce of the puppeteer's arm lowers the puppet slightly more than the preceding bounce. The exits are slightly different for rod arm and human hand and arm puppets. When rod arm puppets exit, the puppeteer should turn the puppet toward his body, swing 180 degrees away from the stage, and exit down the stairs. (If the puppet is on the right hand, the puppeteer turns to his left and then moves away from the stage. He moves to his right if the puppet is on the left hand.) It is important to include depth (18-24 inches of horizontal movement) in walking on or off the stage. Vertical movement without depth makes the puppet appear to be coming up an elevator. At the same time, moving the puppet horizontally without sufficient "bounce" makes the puppet appear to arrive on an escalator. A combination of both is essential for good entrances and exits.

Walking across the stage is similar to entering and exiting. The puppeteer makes short, brief bounces to move the puppet. Again, the emphasis is on making the puppet appear as natural as possible. If the script calls for the puppet to run, speed up the movements; puppets can come close to flying in these instances. The good puppeteer can make a puppet pitch forward and dip below stage level while it is moving across the stage. This is a good technique both for puppets in a hurry or for a puppet whose personality calls for clumsiness.

The entrances and exits of human hand and arm puppets differ slightly from those of rod arm puppets. Because human hand and arm puppets are frequently

These two illustrations show two other incorrect ways of getting the puppet on stage. The first drawing shows the "escalator" entrance, there is not bouncing of the puppet to create a walking effect. The second entrance is called the "elevator;" this is incorrect because it does not use enough horizontal movement when the puppet comes into view. Neither the escalator or elevator entrances appear natural to the audience.

manipulated by two puppeteers, it is not possible to rotate the puppet to a full 180 degrees before exiting. Exits with these puppets should be made by turning 90 degrees in the direction of the free hand of the puppeteer manipulating the mouth. If he uses his right hand in the puppet, the exit should be made parallel to the stage after rotating 90 degrees to the left.

Another important aspect of staging is good eye contact. Human speakers who address audiences must maintain eye contact if they want to maintain the attention of the group. Puppets are no different.

Eye contact is essential for the puppet to maintain during the performance. This is especially important when talking, either to a person as shown, or to another puppet.

Puppets on stage, after all, are supposed to be regarded as real personalities and they must act like them. This is a factor which is scarcely noticed by the audience unless it is absent. If puppets do not look at the audience, it is distracting and detracts from the realism of the production. Since puppet stages are approximately 4 to 4½ feet high, the puppets are generally higher than the audience. This means that the puppeteer must bend his wrist slightly to make the puppets look down on the audience. Otherwise, they will look over the heads of everyone. The puppeteer will also want to know the size of his audience, and how close to and far from, the stage they are. It is also important to know the limits of the audience to either side of the stage. If the puppeteer has this information he can "sweep" over the audience as would any good speaker.

With these words on eye contact must come a cautionary note. The puppet should maintain eye contact only when he directly addresses the audience or is called upon to do so by the script. Otherwise, puppets should speak to each other. Nothing is more distracting and unnatural than a puppet talking to another puppet without looking at it. If the content of the conversation merits, either puppet may turn briefly toward the audience and show its reaction to what is being said — as long as the reactions do not detract from anything of importance which is being said. The puppet director should closely watch his puppeteers to make sure the rules are being followed.

As puppeteers become more experienced with their puppets they will be able to create more impressions by use of the gestures and movements. As a general rule, these gestures need to be overdone in order to communicate their meaning. Fear, for example, cannot be expressed by a puppet which quivers slightly. The

This illustration shows the correct distance which puppets should remain from the stage. The puppet should not be too close to the stage or it will not appear natural to the audience.

puppet that is afraid must literally shake itself to death. Gestures intended to relay an emotional feeling must be exaggerated.

Another important consideration is positioning of the puppets. Be careful not to crowd them too closely together. If a musical number is being performed, or something else which requires movement, the puppets should have sufficient room to move without difficulty. Puppets which sing need to have room to move to both sides, keeping in time to the beat of the music.

The puppeteers must be organized backstage. This drawing illustrates not only the puppet team but the people operating the sound and lighting systems. Puppeteers must thoroughly rehearse their backstage activities to insure a smoothly running show.

This barbershop quartet shows the correct spacing of puppets on stage. Puppets should not be too crowded together.

Experience and experimentation will serve as instructors for puppeteers as they seek to develop staging techniques which find favorable audience response. The sooner these techniques are developed, the better the puppet production will be. Puppeteers must make their puppets come to life; they must animate them. A puppet show without action, movement and gestures is a dull show to watch. Make sure that your puppeteers excite their audiences with active and artistic puppetry.

9

Care, Storage, And Transportation

A great deal has already been said about the necessary preparation and training which is required if the puppeteer is to be capable of performing high quality puppet productions. But there is an additional variable which significantly influences the success of a puppet show — the puppet itself. Unfortunately, some puppet teams have attended training seminars conducted by professional puppeteers, have realized the potential benefits of organizing a puppet team, and have then proceeded to organize without professional quality puppets — selecting toy puppets instead — with the result that the puppeteer's enthusiasm waned and the team never had a real opportunity to succeed.

Puppeteers tend to perform to the level of the puppet itself. A sub-quality, toy puppet is usually manipulated like a toy. But professional puppets seem to bring out the best in puppeteers and the added work

Cradling the puppet over the arm is the best way to carry it. Never pick a puppet up by its arms, ears, or nose.

on the part of the puppeteer results in higher quality shows.

Professional quality puppets are individually hand-crafted and need to be treated with care. Like any other item, puppets will give longer use if they are properly treated. Therefore, the following hints should be valuable for your puppet team in extending the life of its puppets.

1. Puppets are made from various materials which can be soiled. Skin, hair, and clothing must all be treated to protect the puppet; this should be done immediately after your puppets arrive. The easiest way to accomplish this is to thoroughly spray each puppet with Scotch Guard® fabric protector. If the puppet has plastic eyes, they should either be covered during treatment or wiped clean afterwards.

2. Great care should be given the treatment of puppets during use. Puppets should never be tossed around or placed where they might be accidentally stepped on. The puppet team should be organized and thoroughly rehearsed in back-stage procedures so the puppets are well-treated during the show. Fast moving numbers and quick changes of puppets are no excuses for neglecting your puppets.

3. Puppets should never be picked up by their noses, ears, arms, hair, or clothing. This might cause the fabric to stretch or tear. Puppets should only be picked up by the neck; they can be carried either with the puppeteer's hand in place or by placing the puppet head over the puppeteer's arm. If, through normal wear or carelessness, small tears occur in the puppet skin, they can be mended by hand. Get the thread which most closely matches your puppet's skin.

4. Occasionally eyes or eyebrows may come lose. A
    good contact cement or spray adhesive can be
    used to replace them. Be careful not to get glue on
    the puppet where it will show.
5. Inexperienced puppeteers often grab or bite things
    with the mouth of the puppet. This should never
    be done. Biting will cause the mouth to wear badly
    around the edges, prematurely wearing out the
    puppet.
6. Even with Scotch Guard® treatment, puppets will
    become soiled during normal use. Professional
    puppets cannot be washed or dry cleaned because
    the foam parts would deteriorate badly. When
    cleaning becomes necessary, use a good spot
    remover or foam rug cleaner. Brand names which
    have proved effective are K2R® spot remover and
    Woolite® foam rug cleaner.
7. Caution must be exercised when making costume
    changes. Pulling shirts or other clothing up over
    the head may damage the puppet — it should
    never be done. To change costumes quickly and
    efficiently, simply remove the foam body, pull the
    arms out of the sleeves, and slide the garment
    down off the puppet.

To a large extent, the proper care of puppets is a
matter of common sense. If all puppeteers are taught
and understand that their puppets are not playthings
but rather are valuable entertainers and teachers, then
they will be more inclined to treat them correctly. The
care of puppets is a tremendously important aspect of a
successful puppet team.

Puppet storage is another concern which demands
attention. If puppets are stored incorrectly they will not
remain in good condition. Once again, the puppet
team must be aware that their puppets are not toys

which can be tossed in a box after using them. One of the main causes of puppet damage is improper storage.

There are three excellent methods of protecting your puppets during storage. Each has its strong points. The first method is the rack. If the puppet team has a permanent storage area for its equipment, such as a room or large closet, the storage rack is ideal. The rack is simply a rail or pipe upon which the puppets can be placed. The puppet team which uses a PVC pipe and curtain stage (described in chapter 21) can use the stage as a storage rack. Simply place the chin of the puppet over the pipe and it will remain in position, with head on one side of the pipe and body on the other. When all the puppets are in place, a sheet or plastic drop cloth is put over the rack to protect the puppets from dust, dirt, etc. The storage rack can also be constructed of wooden doweling or even a tightly drawn cord. The major disadvantage of this method is its lack of portability. If the puppet team travels

Puppets can be stored on a storage rack made from pipe or doweling. They rest with their chins over the rack and should be covered wuth plastic to be kept clean.

For display purposes, or storage, puppets can be placed on a wooden stand made of doweling and a square base. If just storage is the objective, they should be covered with a plastic bag.

frequently, both puppets and prop rack (if it also serves as the stage) must be packed into other containers to be transported. This might well mean additional preparation time for the team. More mobile teams may wish to consider another method.

The second way of storing puppets is not what is generally thought of as storage. In this method the puppets are placed on stands and can be displayed, an excellent way to promote the puppet team. Puppet stands also serve as a clever way to decorate your office or den. Construction of the stand is simple. The only materials required are a short length of wooden doweling or plastic pipe and an 8" square board. The diameter of the pipe or doweling should be at least

3/4" to make sure it is sturdy enough. Both PVC pipe and doweling are inexpensively obtained at most hardware stores. Drill a hole equal to the diameter of the pipe in the center of the board and place the pipe upright in it. Then insert the pipe into the body and head of the puppet and your puppet stand is complete. If you choose to use this method of storage partly for the decoration, make sure the puppet body and clothing reach the board so that the pipe does not show. A clothespin placed on the inside of the mouth to close it will also give a more natural appearance. If the puppet stand is not used as decoration, each puppet should be covered to keep it clean. This method, like the rack, is not conducive to the team which travels extensively.

The puppet team which is constantly performing in various locations would do well to store their puppets in the same containers used to transport them. The containers should be sturdy, since they will be moved around, and the puppets must not be damaged in transit. Trunks are ideally suited because they are large and durable. Suitcases are sufficient for smaller groups but boxes should be used only if they are strong enough to withstand the punishment of packing and shipping. If trunks, suitcases, or boxes are used, be careful to avoid damage to the puppet heads; they are constructed of foam and can be crushed if packed too tightly. The following instructions are helpful for all puppet teams which will travel to perform puppet productions.

1. Detach the rods from rod-arm puppets.
2. Fold the arms across the chest of the puppet.
3. Roll the puppet up, starting at the bottom of the shirt and moving up to the neck.
4. Place the rolled puppet in the shipping container, alternating the direction in which the heads are

pointed. This will also keep the puppet heads from being crushed.

5. If the puppets do not fill up the container, use sheets of foam or some other lightweight material to fill the empty space and keep the puppets from tossing about during handling.

6. When packing your car or van, do not place heavy objects on the puppet containers if they cannot hold the weight. Speakers or other fairly heavy objects can damage the puppets if they fall on the packing boxes.

7. Make sure the shipping containers are clean! Empty boxes often attract trash and puppets should never be stored where they can pick up dirt or oil stains.

The method of storage you choose depends upon your situation. All have advantages and disadvantages. But the most important consideration involved is the protection of the puppet. Let your imagination and particular needs guide your decision.

Puppets are easily transported. Fold the arms across the chest and roll up the puppet. Then put them carefully into a suitcase, trunk, or sturdy box. Avoid overpacking which might damage the foam heads.

10

Single Puppeteer Performances

Occasionally it is either necessary or desirable to have a single puppeteer perform instead of an entire puppet team. This is quite possible for the accomplished puppeteer and can be done in two possible ways. The first involves the puppeteer being hidden from view behind the stage — as is the custom for puppet shows. The second single puppeteer method allows the puppeteer to remain in view of the audience and perform in similar fashion to a ventriloquist. Both of these methods have proven successful in use and both have particular advantages and disadvantages.

The main advantage of both methods is the ability to perform without the necessity of scheduling and organizing a number of puppet team members. In most learning programs where puppets are used as supplemental instructors, it is necessary to change constantly the pace to keep from having the program

Any prop can be used as a stage for the puppet and puppeteer, as long as it restricts the view of the audience. Television cameras, pulpits, or bookshelves make ideal stages.

become too familiar and boring. Churches and schools are two examples of organizations which must constantly modify their programs to "keep ahead of the game." Unless there are several large and well-disciplined puppet teams within the church or school, it is difficult to sustain a puppet program of high quality that can perform as frequently as desired. The single puppeteer production allows the teacher or some other energetic leader to practice and perform when the puppet team is unavailable.

Another significant use of the single puppeteer performance is closely related to the development of the puppet personality. Younger audiences often relate well to a specific puppet who assumes the role of master of ceremonies, song leader, best friend, or whatever. The single puppeteer can use his puppet to develop this rapport with the audience, a rapport which will aid the entire program even if the puppet only briefly performs. It is not difficult for the puppeteer to perform frequently in this manner, without the necessity for extensive rehearsals. The single puppeteer method of performing is an excellent vehicle for the beginning puppeteer or for those who are unable to enlist the support of enough other individuals to establish a larger puppet group.

1. PUPPETEER CONCEALED FROM VIEW. This method is the traditional technique for puppets. A full stage is required to block the audience's view of the puppeteer. Sound, lip sync, staging, and the puppet's personality remain the same — as if the production were by a puppet team. Obviously, the single puppeteer performance limits the number of puppets which can be used at one time, although scripts can be written to have some characters appear briefly on stage and then exit.

A single puppeteer can use two puppets for a performance. Rod arms hang naturally down the puppet's sides.

The puppeteer then switches puppets behind stage. Otherwise, only two puppets can be used, and this only with an experienced puppeteer. As a general rule, single puppeteer productions should restrict themselves to the use of just one puppet.

Although many single puppeteer shows consist of one puppet and a monologue, it is possible to establish a dialog with another person. This is an excellent method of establishing a relationship between a puppet friend and an adult, from which many learning experiences can occur. In this technique, the natural conversations between two "friends" can present countless situations in which the audience can identify and learn.

2.   THE PUPPETEER IN VIEW. The second method of performing with just one puppeteer is to have the puppeteer remain in view of the audience. This is sometimes necessary if it is a classroom situation where the only adult present is the puppeteer. In control purposes, the puppeteer must be able to maintain eye contact with the students. This need for control *restricts* the puppeteer from the traditional backstage performance.

The puppeteer performing in view of the audience cannot use a human hand and arm puppet. A rod arm or hand only puppet must be used. To perform with the puppeteer in view of the audience, it is necessary to have some type of adequate prop which conceals the lower puppet body and the arm of the puppeteer which manipulates the puppet. Suitable props include pianos, desks, book shelves, television cameras, even puppet stages! The audience must never see the puppeteer's arm extending from the puppet's body. This destroys the effect of presenting the was discussed in the chapter on the puppet personality. From his position of viewing both Personality. From his position of viewing both puppet and audience, the puppeteer can speak to both. He can carry on a conversation first with one and then with the other.

How is this done? The most important point to remember is that, although the positioning of the puppeteer is similar to that of a ventriloquist, the puppeteer is *not* a ventriloquist and *should not attempt to speak for the puppet.* The puppeteer speaks *to* the puppet. The puppet's responses to the conversation need to be pre-recorded on

A desk makes an ideal stage for a performance where the puppeteer must remain in view of the audience.

cassette tape. This requires advance planning and preparation but is extremely entertaining and effective. The creative puppeteer will even be able to inject ad-lib comments into the program without deviating from the thrust of the script or pre-recorded tape. In preparing for this method of performing with a single puppeteer, the following steps are helpful to consider:

a. Determine the content of the production and write the exact dialog for both puppet and puppeteer. It is extremely important to have a complete, written script before recording.

b. Pre-record the puppet's part of the conversation or song. Make sure a distinct voice is used for the puppet and that this voice remains consistent each time the puppet performs. Do not leave lengthy gaps in the tape where the puppeteer will speak. Attempting to synchronize these gaps to the estimated time of the puppeteer's part only creates timing difficulties during the actual production. Instead, leave just a one or two second gap between sections of the puppet's pre-recorded conversation.

c. The puppeteer should speak into a live microphone during the actual performance. This matches the amplified tone of the recording and makes the entire conversation more realistic.

d. When the script calls for the puppet to speak, the tape is broadcast. It is stopped at the end of each segment to allow the puppeteer to insert his comments. Starting and stopping the tape is easy to do by using the remote control "on-off" switch on the microphone. Most cassette recorders have this feature. The puppeteer can thus hold the microphone switch out of sight in his free hand, simply switching it on or off whenever the script requires. The brief pauses between recorded segments make it easier for the puppeteer to establish the correct timing and correctly begin the lip sync on the first syllable of the first word in the sentence.

Some remote control switches with cassette recorders cannot be operated without an audible "click" sound which is noticeable to the audience. If this is the case, an alternative method must be used. If a more sophisticated cassette deck is used, one which has a pause button, the puppeteer can have an assistant operate the recorder, leaving adequate pauses for the puppeteer to speak his lines. Unfortunately, however, this option is not available for many teams.

The remaining alternative requires practice and perfect timing. This method consists of leaving blank tape between the puppet's lines which correspond exactly to the length of the puppeteer's comments. In this method, there is no room for error as the pre-recorded dialog may overlap with the puppeteer's lines. With adequate rehearsals, however, the tape can be left running to allow the single puppeteer performance.

This method is an excellent vehicle for creating learning situations in a classroom or church setting. There is one additional way of using a single puppeteer in a puppet production: using the puppet as a silent participant. This requires a puppeteer who must be skillful at manipulating the puppet's arms, body, and head. In this method, the puppeteer speaks to the puppet, usually asking questions, and the puppet responds with gestures only. Or, the puppet can appear to whisper answers in the puppeteer's ear and have him relay the answers to the audience. (The puppet mouth must open as if whispering.) The silent puppet is capable of displaying a wide range of emotions: fear, joy, sadness, timidity, etc. It is one of the more difficult phases of puppetry, but one which the skillful puppeteer will want to attempt.

The performance with a single puppeteer adds to the versatility of any puppet team or individual puppeteer. Like any other type of performance, it requires discipline, practice and creativity. The quality puppet team will want to include this technique in its repertoire.

This puppeteer is seated in such a way that his arm in the puppet is concealed by his body. Single puppeteer shows with the audience in view can use any props available to block the audience's view of the puppeteer's arm.

11

Variety Puppet Shows

Quality puppetry is entertaining, one of the best forms of entertainment in the variety show. This format has been used successfully on television, in clubs, wherever entertainers perform. Puppets, as entertainers, should also be able to perform variety shows and the enthusiastic puppet team, regardless of its organizational affiliation, will want to have variety programming in its repertoire.

In recent years one of the major failures in puppetry has been the scheduling of long, drawn-out productions which are unable to maintain the interest of the audience. In these productions, sometimes 45 minutes to one hour in length, the puppets are used as characters in extended plays. Often the entire production consists of one play with several different acts. This format is not well-suited to puppets. It dulls the basic effectiveness of the puppet by destroying its novelty.

The audience soon becomes familiar with the puppet and the play and attentions wander.

Puppet performances are only as successful as the formats in which they are presented. Bright, enthusiastic, stimulating puppets cannot maintain these qualities if forced into a dull format. For this reason, the format of a puppet show must be given ample consideration. Experience has shown that such consideration will result in a variety format which utilizes brief, hard-hitting segments which are constantly changing so that every few minutes the audience is being presented with something new. This principle of presentation holds true despite the basic orientation of the puppet team.

The church puppet team, for example, will perform puppet productions which present the basic truths of their particular religious persuasion. This may mean that much of the puppet programming will be oriented toward teaching truths of the Bible. The content of this team, however, must be presented in a format similar to that of the school team instructing students in the three R's. That is, the productions must vary in the method of presentation; these must be brief segments, ones which do not allow the audience to drift because they lack entertainment. Some basic rules exist concerning the length of puppet plays, rules which must not be violated if the audience is to remain entertained. Generally speaking, plays for primary-aged children (grades 1-3) should never be longer than six minutes. Grades 4-6 are reasonably capable of viewing a 6-8 minute show and junior high-aged students can sometimes sit comfortably from 10-12 minutes. Plays for high school students and adults can be up to 15 minutes in length. No single puppet play should ever be longer than 15 minutes — it is best to be on the safe side and have the play end too soon rather than too late. Also, it will need to be remembered that the longer the play, the greater the need for humor and change of pace within the play.

Variety shows consist of several little "mini-plays" within the overall production. Musical numbers, humorous routines, and short skits should all be interspersed to keep the action moving. An example of a variety show performed in a church setting is given below. Notice the brief amount of time allotted for each segment.

1. Welcome and introductions by Master of Ceremonies — 2 minutes
2. Hilarious musical number by people or animal puppets — 2 minutes
3. Live dialog between the puppets and one puppeteer standing in front of the stage. Or conversation between puppets and audience — 3 minutes
4. Humorous comedy, song, or dialog routine — 3 minutes
5. Introduction of main skit by Master of Ceremonies — 1 minute
6. Song which communicates the essence of the main skit — 2 minutes
7. Main skit — 10 minutes
8. A happy song to leave the audience on the up-beat — 2 minutes

A close look at the program in chapter 13 shows that despite its variety and change in presentation technique, it still is a unified presentation, revolving around the main skit. School teams or those formed strictly with an entertaining emphasis may substitute a play of their own choosing for this one, which presents a Bible truth. The result is still a series of performances designed to capture and maintain the attention of the audience. A note of caution needs to be given to all puppet teams at this point. Each time they present a play more than five minutes in length, it should reflect the same basic features of the overall variety show. That is, it should contain changes of pace, music, humor, or other techniques which are designed to entertain.

Some additional recommendations may be helpful in your preparation for a variety show. For a show approximately 20-30 minutes long, it may be necessary to have two puppet teams if the puppeteers are relatively inexperienced. A small puppet team that is not used to performing extended shows will find it difficult to maintain arm control for an entire half hour. Using larger teams, or two small teams, allows the puppeteers to alternate members and rest their arms. The variety format is excellent for such trades since there are many transition periods during the show. Puppeteers can trade places during this interval, and can also serve a useful purpose in helping with puppets, props, tapes and other accessories organized backstage.

When planning the variety show, the director should arrange the various segments with transitions in mind. Adequate time should be allowed, but it is best to keep the intervals between segments as short as possible. The sequence of segments should also be arranged so that the different styles of puppetry which may accompany changes in puppeteers is not too noticeable. The best way to accomplish this is to change the content at the same time puppeteers are changed, such as from a comedy number to a musical number.

The discipline of the puppet team is a critical factor when performing a variety show. The puppeteers must be thoroughly rehearsed and well-organized backstage in order to make the show flow smoothly. All of the necessary materials, and the puppeteers, should be in place backstage before the audience arrives. It is extremely unprofessional and distracting to see people coming and going from behind the stage. Another distracting aspect of variety shows which can result if the puppet team is not prepared is voices and noises heard backstage between or during performances. The audience should never see or hear a puppeteer until after the performance is complete.

One way to provide a smooth transition from one sequence to the next is through the use of pre-recorded music. In fact, the entire show, including transition music, should be pre-recorded to help the show flow smoothly. Having the entire program on a master tape also eliminates frantic last-minute searches for lost cassettes. If part of the performance is to be given live, the tape can be stopped and then started again when the recorded sequences are ready to resume.

Puppet teams that insist on quality will be asked to perform in a wide variety of settings: church groups, service clubs, civic organizations, and many more. It is possible to create the basic format variety show which can be slightly modified to fit any audience. And, once learned, the variety show will prove a useful tool for the puppet team that is being sought by organizations for performance dates.

12

Live And Pre-recorded Performances

Puppets have an innate ability to entertain and communicate with an audience. Their novelty, the puppeteer's ability, and well-written scripts all contribute to their ability. But by themselves these factors are not enough; puppets are not artists of pantomine. The puppet must be able to communicate the spoken word. Puppet teams may choose one of two methods to perform the sound for their productions. The two basic methods are performing the sound live or pre-recording the script for playback during the performance.

Pre-recorded plays are easier for beginning puppeteers to perform since they allow the puppeteer to concentrate strictly on puppet manipulations. For the inexperienced puppeteer, this is a great advantage over coordinating both live dialog and manipulation. Pre-recording the puppet play also provides a consistent, high quality sound for the production. In addition to the dialog itself, musical interludes, background, and sound effects can be incorporated into the pre-recorded tape. Pre-recording puppet plays also provides a valuable outlet for many technically-oriented young people who might not express the necessary creativity for a puppeteer. These individuals can provide much-needed assistance handling the details and technical aspects of the recording sessions.

Most groups of young people contain several who have a keen interest in recording. These individuals can often set up a miniature recording studio and produce a sophisticated product. There are several important steps, however, which must be observed before record-ing the actual tape.

1. Copies of the script should be duplicated and distributed to those who will read the various parts. Some ad-lib changes may result during the session but it is highly unusual for good changes to result. Do not try to record a play spontaneously; a written script is necessary.

2. Rehearsal is necessary here, just as in all other phases of quality puppetry. The play should be read through several times before taping to familiarize the readers with it.

3. Some thought should be given beforehand to considerations such as voice tones, number and length of pauses between lines, etc. The readers should imagine how the script will be performed so the sound track complements the puppets' per-formances and allows them sufficient time to develop their personalities. Adequate pauses should be given for entrances, exits and other movements.

    Voices should be selected to fit the personality of the puppet represented and should be consistent throughout the play. It is also important to maintain uniform sound levels so the audience is not distracted with too loud and too soft fluctuations in the sound track.

4. Voices must sound natural. The reader must be familiar enough with the script to insure that the dialog does not sound like it is being read. The performance, after all, is not that of puppets reading to each other but rather they are speaking in a conversational tone. Also, it is important that voices be easily distinguishable from each other. Do not confuse the audience by voices which are too similar. It is also extremely important for voices to be understandable. A common fault of puppeteers representing characters of children is that the voices are so juvenile they cannot be understood. Remember, the audience is unfamiliar with the script; each word must be clearly enunciated or the enjoyment of the audience will be significantly decreased. This is very important — sound natural!

5. The taping session itself must be well-organized. Tape recorders, microphones and other necessary equipment should be in place prior to the start of the session. If technical equipment is not in operation when the readers arrive, discipline often breaks down and this is frequently reflected in the quality of the final product. Time is a precious commodity for busy puppet teams! It must be guarded jealously in all phases of puppet-related activity.

Once the recording session is complete, practice can begin with the puppets. At this point, it may be discovered that additional pauses are necessary to permit certain movements on stage. If this is the case, the technical sound man can simply add appropriate lengths of leader tape where they are required.

The puppeteers will need to master the timing of the tape perfectly before the script is performed before an audience. Better yet, the puppeteer should memorize the entire script, both dialog and timing, in order to facilitate the accurate lip sync required. It is also helpful for the puppeteer to follow a written copy of the script during the performance. This will serve the same purpose as do the cue cards used by actors and assist the puppeteer in recalling future lines.

A "live" puppet show is when the puppeteer not only manipulates the puppet behind the stage, but also provides the voice for the puppet. Although some puppeteers cannot seem to master the dual nature of this performance, it does provide certain advantages over the pre-recorded show. Primarily, it allows the show to be adapted to the individual nature of each audience. Experienced puppeteers can design their performance, if necessary, to be more fully enjoyed by the audience. The live show also allows the puppet to interact with the audience during the performance. This technique is highly successful and adds a new dimension to the realism of the puppet production.

The ability to modify a performance to suit the individual audience, however, does not mean that live shows are always spontaneous or unplanned. On the contrary, live shows require planning and written scripts, if they are going to successfully present an instructional message. Quality live shows perhaps require even more rehearsal and planning than do their pre-recorded counterparts since it is more difficult to provide both voices and manipulation. In live shows, there is also a strong need to maintain strict discipline or the content of the performance may degenerate. Puppeteers must be made to understand that puppet shows are performed with a purpose, and ad-lib comments must not be allowed to detract from this overall purpose. The puppet director has the responsibility to critique ad-lib comments and insure that they are tastefully done and add to, rather than detract from, the puppet production. Experience will teach the puppet team about the usefulness and drawbacks of ad-lib commentary.

Several techniques help make the live show especially entertaining. One of these is conversing and maintaining eye contact with specific audience members. For this to happen, the puppeteer must carefully screen the audience before the start of the performance. He should notice how close to and far from the stage they are, and how far to each side the audience extends. Individuals in the audience should be singled out (by name if possible) and distinguishing characteristics noted. During the performance, for example, a puppet may wish to select an individual and carry on a conversation. ("Hi, Nancy! How are you today? That sure is a good looking sweater you're wearing. But who is that funny looking guy sitting next to you?") In doing this, make sure the puppet looks directly at the person with whom it is talking and gestures will also want to be directed at the selected individual. This technique can be used several times during a performance but caution should be exercised to keep from overworking it. Puppet teams should not over-saturate their audiences, they should leave them wanting more.

Live puppets are also capable of dealing with audiences that become slightly unruly, although this is often a sign that the puppets no longer have the attention of the audience and the show should be ended. If immediate measures are unable to correct the situation — such as having the puppets talk directly to

the individuals causing the disturbance — then additional efforts to continue the show should be aban-
doned.

Another technique of experienced puppeteers is of
great benefit during live shows. In these shows, because
more activity is taking place, the chance for mistakes is
greater. The experienced puppeteer will use such
mistakes to his advantage. Don't get upset by mistakes;
if something unexpected occurs, use it to advantage.
This is done simply by capitalizing on the error — by
making it seem as if it were planned. If, for example, a
musical number is being performed by a group of
puppets and one puppet seems to be slightly off, turn
this puppet into the "Sad Sack" of the cast. Include
these mistakes as part of the production by having the
puppet react to his own mistakes. Puppet gestures
which are useful in achieving this effect include the
puppet hitting himself in the head, holding his hand
over his mouth, crying, and looking alternately at the
audience and then at the other puppets. The remaining
puppets will also want to react to the mistake maker. In
this way, mistakes add to the entertainment aspect of
the puppet production.

Both live performances and pre-recorded performances require time and effort to perfect. The good
puppet team should be capable of performing either
method. Which method is used is a matter of individual
preference and the dictates of the particular performance. Whichever method is used, it should be
rehearsed thoroughly enough to guarantee a quality
show.

5. Mr. Quimper and his friends are the cast for a television series
produced by Puppet Productions.

6. Human hand and arm puppets add a new dimension to puppetry. Here grandma and grandpa are joined by a rod arm
oriental and rod arm Indian puppet.

3. A colorful, backstage look at a puppet production. Lighting is important for puppet shows, just as it is for any entertainment mode.

4. Puppet Productions, Inc., of San Diego, California, manufactures a complete line of professional hand puppets. Pictured here are some of the animal puppets which are available.

1. Marionette shows, one of the oldest forms of puppet entertainment, provide a colorful display as well as serving as vehicles for communication.

2. The cast from the educational script "Alcohol on Trial." Four body-part puppets are used in this play to inform viewers about the physiological effects of alcohol.

7. Anglo puppets form a popular set for beginning puppeteers.

8. Puppet Productions also makes Afro and Chicano puppets, in addition to the colorful cartoon characters.

13

Writing Puppet Plays

Script writing is an important aspect of puppetry which cannot be overemphasized. Puppets are, after all, just like any other performers who are dependent on their lines for a successful performance. Star actors and actresses read scripts which are offered them and are quite selective about which ones they choose to perform. They recognize that a quality performance is not enough to overcome a seriously deficient script. Puppets, of course, do not have this advantage. For this reason, it is imperative that the puppet director screen each script and insist upon quality material before allowing it to be performed.

Several factors influence the suitability of a script and must be kept in mind during its development. These factors form an excellent framework within which the creative puppeteer or script writer can fabricate an entertaining program.

1. One of the most important considerations in script
    writing is to insure that the vocabulary is suitable
    for the age level and educational background of
    the audience. Many outstanding scripts contain
    humor which is easily understandable by adults but
    which is lost on children. Such scripts must be
    adapted before they are produced for younger
    audiences. Vocabulary is also frequently used
    which the audience is not able to understand. This
    results in attention shifting away from the puppets
    and the puppet show fails to accomplish its goal.
    Make sure the words and content of the script are
    easily understandable by the audience.

2. Puppets will frequently become behavior models
    for younger audiences. That is, they will often
    imitate the behavior of the puppets or copy the
    vocabulary. It is important, therefore, to realize this
    and write the script accordingly. Violence of any
    sort should not be included in the play if it may
    lead to aggressive behavior by the children. Also,
    phrases and words such as "stupid," "dumb," and
    "shut-up" serve no useful purpose and should not
    be included. This may seem like a trivial point but
    the influence of puppets, like that of television and
    other communications tools, is dramatic and must
    be controlled.

3. The length of the plays is very important. A
    frequent mistake made by many puppet teams is
    the production of plays which seemingly never
    end. When writing puppet plays, always keep in
    mind that the success of puppets lies in their ability
    to command the attention of the audience. Overly
    long plays destroy this ability. It is better to leave
    audiences waiting to see more than to have them
    feel they should have left early. A general rule for
    the length of puppet plays is:

> Primary (grades 1-3) - less than six minutes
> Junior (grades 4-6) - 6-8 minutes
> Junior High - 10-12 minutes
> High School and Adults - up to 15 minutes

4. Length of individual lines is also important within plays. Do not have extended monologues or the audience will become bored and lose interest in the play. Dialog should be brief and stress back-and-forth interaction among the puppet participants.

5. Scripts for puppets must be relatively simple. Do not attempt to become too complex by introducing subplots or involved characters. Each puppet play should be restricted to one theme. Instructional puppetry should not attempt to teach both vowels and numbers in the same play. The two concepts should be separated in different plays and with at least slightly changed formats.

   It is also important for the individual puppet characters to be relatively easy to understand. It is only confusing to the audience to introduce complex personalities into puppet plays.

6. Puppet shows require action. Plays should be written with this in mind. The script writer should visualize on-stage action as the play is being written to insure a good flow of action throughout the play. Caution should be exercised, however, to keep from having competing forms of action on stage at the same time.

7. No more than three or four puppets should be on stage at one time unless musical numbers are being performed. Scripts should be written to have puppets enter and exit in order to keep this maximum number under control.

8. If intermissions are necessary to change sets or puppets, make them as brief as possible to keep from harming the atmosphere created by the puppets. Scripts should be written to keep intermissions to a minimum.

9. When puppet characters are developed for permanent use by a puppet team, the script writers will need to be aware of these personalities in order to consistently present each personality from one play to the next.

Beginning puppet teams may require source material to provide ideas for puppet presentations. This is amply available. Depending on the type of play which is being written, newspapers, children's books, story-telling record albums, textbooks and Bible stories all contain good material for scripts. Additionally, scripts can be adapted for use with puppets which were originally intended for something else, such as flannelgraph scripts. Plays designed specifically for puppets are also published in both written and pre-recorded tape form. Puppet Productions publishes a monthly newsletter with at least four pages of scripts. The material is endless; the creative puppet team will find puppet scripts from almost any situation which occurs in the routine of life.

Examples, however, often teach far better than instructions alone. For this reason, several scripts are given here to illustrate good and bad scripts. Two scripts are printed here as examples for good scripts that have proven tremendously successful in numerous performances. "Short Subjects" is the story of Zacchaeus from the longer play of the same name and based on the Biblical figure. Notice the familiar television show format and the liberal use of humor. Characters are fairly simple and uncomplicated and the central theme of the play is self-image. "Short Subjects" is a good pattern for your scripts.

"Short Subjects"

CAST

```
EMCEE  . . . . . . . . . .Big, booming, friendly voice
ZACCHAEUS  . . . . . . . . . . . . . . . . Nasal voice
MOTHER  . . . . . . .Lower Bronx Jewish slang type
MISS PINECOHEN . . . . . . . . . .Granny type voice
SGT. MALACHI . . . . . . . . . . . . . . . . . .Stern
LION . . . . . . . . . . .Cartoon type voice, friendly
TAXPAYERS . . . . . . . . . . . . . . . . .Off Stage
(MUSIC  . . . . . . . .Organ playing "Zacchaeus Was
    A Wee Little Man")
```

EMCEE Greetings to all you viewers out there. . . We're here today to learn more about another famous person. . . to let you in on the background. . . the "Nitty-Gritty" in a famous life. And so. . . "This Is Your Life". . . Zacchaeus Stein! (FANFARE AND APPLAUSE) Come on up here on stage, Zaccheaus. . . that's right, it's you come on up. . . (ZACK ENTERS SHYLY. . . KEEP PUPPET LOW, HE'S SHORT. . .) Now just turn around here and say "Hi" to all these fine folks in our audience today. . .

ZACK Ah. . . Hi, Folks. . .

EMCEE We want to find out some of the things in your life that led up to that famous encounter with Jesus of Nazareth. . . that event which made you famous in our history and gave you a special mention in the Word of God. . . in Luke, Chapter 19. . .

ZACK Ah, yes. . . that's my favorite chapter. . .

EMCEE I'm sure it is. . . Now we must hurry right along here. Let's start at the very beginning. . .

ZACK A very good place to start. . .

EMCEE Ah, yes. . . I understand that you were born right here in Jericho, is that right?

ZACK SEWN. . .

EMCEE I beg your pardon. . .

ZACK I was SEWN. . . puppets are sewn, not born.

EMCEE I'm sure we are. . . now tell us, Zack, what do you remember about your early childhood?

ZACK Well,. . . actually I don't remember a whole lot. . . I was very young at the time. . .

EMCEE I'm sure you were. . . to fill us in on those early days. . . we've asked your mother to join us. . . (ORGAN FANFARE AND APPLAUSE. THEY EMBRACE)

MOM Hi, Zacky. . . (STANDS BACK AND LOOKS HIM OVER). . . My. . . how you HAVEN'T grown!

ZACK Hi, Mom. . . (UNENTHUSIASTICALLY)

EMCEE We've brought you here today, Mrs. Stein, to tell us all about Zacchaeus' childhood.

MOM Well, that won't take very long.

EMCEE Why not?

MOM Because he's always been short. . . everything about Zacky is short.

EMCEE (LOOKING DOWN AT ZACK) Hmmmm. . . I see what you mean.

MOM He wasn't just short. . . he was super-short. . . Shrimpy in fact. . .

EMCEE Exactly how short was he in those days?

MOM Why, he was so short he couldn't reach the light switch until he was eight years old. He slept in his baby bed until he was 12. In restaurants he'd always go from table to table, collecting used gum wads from under each table. You know what I mean?

EMCEE Uh huh! Well, tell us, how did you and your husband help him adjust to being so short?

MOM I used to say to him. . . "Zacky, you're short". . . and his dad would say, "Zack, you're sure a little pip squeak". . . and, of course, the other children helped out a lot too. . .

EMCEE And how did they do that?

MOM Oh, they called him names and teased him a lot. . . we had a lovely family. . .

EMCEE I'm sure you did. Well, we thank you for joining us today, Mrs. Stein.

MOM Oh, that's okay, I didn't have anything to do anyway, cuties. By the way, I have four other. . . "Regular" children. . . I'd love to tell you about them someday. . .

EMCEE I'm sure you would. . . Bye, bye now.

ZACK Bye, Mom.

MOM Bye, Zacky. . . and don't forget to take your vitamins. . . (EXITS LAUGHING)

EMCEE Now that we know a little about Zack's home life. . . let's find out about him as a student. (ZACK TURNS AND TRIES TO SNEAK AWAY) Oh, now Zack, you come back here. We've brought Miss Pinecohen, your 7th grade teacher at Jericho Junior High School, here to fill us in on those wonderful school years. (ORGAN MUSIC. . . MISS PINECOHEN ENTERS WEARING BIG

GLASSES. . .OBVIOUSLY CAN'T SEE TOO WELL.) Welcome to "This Is Your Life," Miss Pinecohen.

MISS P (HUGGING EMCEE) Glad to be here, sir. . . Hello, Zacchaeus. . .

EMCEE Ah. . . no, ma'am. . . Zack is over there. . .

ZACK Hi, Miss Pincohen. . . Ah, over here ma'am. . .

MISS P I'm afraid I don't see too well these days.

EMCEE Our viewers want to hear some of the highlights of Zacchaeus' school days. . . did you know him well?

MISS P Oh, I should say so. . . why, I used to bring him my old Sears catalogs to sit on, so he could see over the top of his desk. The only really big highlight came when little Zacky finally made the baseball team. He was so excited when he told me. . . he ran over and kissed my kneecap.

EMCEE Was he the pitcher?

MISS P No. . . the short-stop. . . He was very short you know. . .

EMCEE Yes, I know, we just talked to his mother. Well, thanks so much for being here today, Miss Pinecohen. Bye, bye, for now. . .

MISS P Bye, Zack. . . Zack, where are you? (LOOKS AROUND BLINDLY. . . FINALLY DOWN TO ZACK) Oh. . . there you are. . . I'll be through with this year's catalog in a month or two. . .

ZACK Thanks, Miss Pinecohen. . . Bye. . .

EMCEE Well, Zack, what did you think about most during your school years?

ZACK Worms.

EMCEE Worms!??

ZACK Worms.

EMCEE Well, what about worms?

ZACK Nobody loves me, everybody hates me — I'm gonna eat worms.

EMCEE Do you mean to say that you felt unloved, rejected?

ZACK No, I felt short.

EMCEE Oh, I'm sure you did. Now we have Sgt. Malachi of the Jericho Marine Recruiting Office. (SGT. ENTERS AND SALUTES) Welcome, Sgt. Malachi. (ORGAN BRIDGE) Would you tell us, sir, about Zacchaeus' military service?

SGT. Yeah, yeah. It was short.

EMCEE Short?

SGT. Yeah, short. . . I sent him to boot camp one day. . . and they sent him back the next.

EMCEE What seemed to be the problem?

SGT. Well, he was SO short. . . that the only uniform they could find to fit him was a boy scout uniform. . . then he kept rubbing two sticks together and starting fire. . . (STARTS TO SING) little fires here. . . little fires there. . . here a fire. . . there a fire. . . everywhere a fire-fire. . . little Zacky set a fire-e-eye O. . . (AS HE SINGS HE EXITS. . . SOUND OF SONG FADES OUT. . .)

EMCEE Well, Zack, what did you do after you failed as a marine?

ZACK I tried to get a job in the Circus. . .

EMCEE Ah yes. . . and to tell us about that. . . The KING of the Beasts. . . (APPLAUSE) Welcome to the show, King. (ORGAN MUSIC. . . LION

ROARS) Easy with that stuff. . . we have a lot of children here today. . . Now tell us, King, what happened when Zack applied for a job in the circus?

LION Well, the long and the short of it is. . . he didn't get the job.

EMCEE Was he by chance, too small?

LION No, no, not too small. . . he was too TALL.

EMCEE Did you hear that folks. . . he was too TALL. . . Why was he too tall?

LION He wanted to be a midget, but he was too tall.

EMCEE I see, well thank you for sharing that with us today, King, so long for now. (LION EXITS ROARING) Well, Zack. . . after all of those disappointments. . . what did you finally decide to do with your life?

ZACK I just became a Tax Collector - they don't have to be tall - just "GREEDY."

EMCEE Now let's have a word from some of the taxpayers. . . (OFF STAGE. . . BOO, BOO BOOOOOOOO) I see you didn't make a whole lot of friends.

ZACK None at all, but I made a lot of money.

EMCEE Yes, I'm sure you did. Now, did all the money make you happy?

ZACK No, I was still unhappy, and still short.

EMCEE Well, tell us what happened then?

ZACK One day, as I was just standing around being short, Jesus came walking by. There were thousands of people in the way and I couldn't see

Him. So I climbed up in a big, old sycamore tree to get a better look.

EMCEE Did you see Him?

ZACK Yes, yes, and He saw me! He told me to come down.

EMCEE Did He want to make fun of you for being so short?

ZACK No, no! He wanted to come to my house and tell me how much God loved me, and how much He loved me. Nobody ever said they loved me before.

EMCEE Nobody? Ever?

ZACK Nobody! Ever! All anyone ever said to me was, 'Zacchaeus, you're short.' Well, right then and there I accepted Jesus as my Savior and I've been happy ever since.

EMCEE And did that change your life?

ZACK Did it ever! Why, I even paid those taxpayers back four times what I took from them. (TAXPAYERS OFF STAGE — "YEA — YEA — YEA") Little kids in Sunday school even sing a song about me being so short. But I don't care a bit, 'cause it helps people learn that Jesus loves them, too, even if they're short, or tall, or fat, or skinny, or have freckles or big noses; even if nobody likes them or even if everyone else likes them — Jesus loves them most of all! Say. . . could we sing my song?

EMCEE Why, sure. . . come on all you kids out there, join in. . . (INTRO TO ZACK'S SONG STARTS UNDER THIS DIALOGUE) (SONG) (AFTER SONG) Well, kids. . . that's about all the time we have for today's show. . . Let's all say a big "Good-bye" to Zacchaeus Stein.

ZACK Bye, by all you guys and gals. . . Bye, bye. (CURTAIN CLOSES AND MUSIC CONTINUES UNDER ABOVE DIALOG . . . THEN MUSIC FADES OUT)

Notice the brief lines and constant interaction in "Short Subjects." There is no need to have one puppet say everything all at one. This only detracts from the show.

"It's On The House" is a brief script designed to help children understand the importance of being kind to each other. Like "Short Subjects," it contains few lengthy dissertations but wisely chooses to instruct through the dialog of the various characters.

It's On The House

CAST MR. QUIMPER, HERB, SKIP & PRISCILLA

SCENE Mr. Quimper working in the soda shoppe, enter Herb and Skip. Mr. Quimper is singing to himself first line of "The Happy Side of Life." Herb and Skip are seated at counter.

MR. Q La, la, la, la, la, la, la, la, la. . . There we go. . . now, let's see. . . Oh, hi, boys. Gettin' pretty hot out there?

SKIP Boy, you can say that again. I haven't been this hot since my electric blanket short-circuited last year.

MR. Q Ha, ha, ha. . . Well, what can I do for you fellas?

SKIP I'll have a large root beer float.

HERB Yeah, and I'll have the same. I love root beer.

MR. Q Comin' right up. . . seems like everybody's favorite today is root beer. That makes 47. . . no, 48 root beer floats I've sold today. (Serves their floats.)

HERB Wow! When it's hot this place sure does a lot of business.

SKIP Yeah. . . Boy, this is just what I needed. Hey, look! Here comes Priscilla. (Priscilla enters, and joins the boys at the counter.)

PRISCILLA Oh, so here you guys are! What are you doin' anyway?

HERB Sitting down. . .

SKIP Havin' a float. . .

HERB Breathin'. . .

SKIP Talkin' to you. . .

PRISCILLA Okay, okay! I shouldn't have asked.

MR. Q Oh, Priscilla! How're you?

PRISCILLA Hot! I came in for a float too.

MR. Q Don't tell me. . . root beer. . .

PRISCILLA Right! The biggest one you've got, Mr. Quimper.

MR. Q Well, you're in luck. I've got just enough root beer for just one more. (Mr. Quimper prepares Priscilla's float. Skip begins to slurp his drink.)

HERB Hey, Skip, quit slurpin' your float. (Skip looks up at Herb, who then begins to drink his own float slurping. Skip shows aggravation and returns to his float.)

MR. Q Here you are, Priscilla. The biggest root beer float I've got.

PRISCILLA Wow! (Priscilla takes straw in mouth and begins to drink.)

HERB Hey! We've gotta' get back to the baseball game.

SKIP Yeah! It might be my turn at bat by now. (As the boys are leaving the counter, Herb knocks Priscilla's float to the floor.)

HERB Uh, oh!

PRISCILLA Oh, no! My float! Boo-hoo, boo-hoo!

HERB Oh, I'm sorry Priscilla. I'll buy you another one. Give her another one, Mr. Quimper.

MR. Q I'm out of root beer, Herb. How about coke?

PRISCILLA Oh, my, no! I don't like coke. I'm allergic, or something. It makes me break out in splotches. . . PURPLE splotches!

SKIP Oh, what're you gonna' do now, Herb?

HERB (Reluctantly) Uh, well, oh gee, here, Priscilla. You can have MY float. I like coke. . . sometimes.

PRISCILLA I don't know. . . Are you sure? (Herb acknowledges with gesture.)

PRISCILLA Thank you, Herb.

MR. Q One large coke float comin' up.

HERB Here's the money, Mr. Quimper.

SKIP There goes your hot dog after the game.

MR. Q Keep your money, Herb. This one's on the house. Just make sure it's not "on the house" like the first one is.

HERB You mean I get this one free?

MR. Q That's right, Herb. You showed me that you learned a very important lesson.

HERB What's that?

MR. Q Well, how to be kind to each other. That's something all of us need to practice.

PRISCILLA That's right.

HERB I know. But sometimes it's not easy to be kind.

MR. Q No, it's not. But you can always ask God to help you.

HERB Yeah, I guess so.

SKIP Hey, come on. I'm gonna lose my turn at bat.

HERB Okay, okay. I'm comin'! Bye, Mr. Quimper. . . and thanks.

MR. Q So long boys. (Herb and Skip start to leave.)

PRISCILLA I better be going too, Mr. Quimper. I'm up after Skip.

MR. Q You mean the boys let you play?

PRISCILLA LET me? I'm the captain of the team.

SKIP Yeah, she's the best. Come on, Priscilla, you gotta' hit us a HOME RUN. (They all exit. Mr. Quimper gestures confusion, then resumes his song.)

MR. Q La, la, la, la, la, la, la, la, la.

An excellent educational script is "Guess That
Vowel." The play is simple and does not attempt to
force too much into one play. Again, pay particular
attention to the television format with which school
children can readily identify. This familiarity is an instant
aid in getting their attention.

Guess That Vowel
CAST

GENE SUNBURN . . . . A typical T.V. Host
MR. A.E. OWENS . . . . A typical contestant
MRS Eunice "I" . . . . A typical contestant
JOHNNY . . . . .An announcer offstage
(SHORT MUSICAL INTRODUCTION)

JOHNNY And now, it's time to play. . . Guess That
    Vowel! (APPLAUSE) Here's the star of our
    show. . . Gene Sunburn! (APPLAUSE)

GENE SUNBURN Hello, there, and here are our two
    contestants for today's game. Contestant Number
    One is a businessman from Ohio, Mr. A E. Owens.
    (ENTER MR. OWENS.)

MR. OWENS Hi, Mom.

GENE SUNBURN . . . and from Los Angeles comes
    Contestant Number Two, Mrs. Eunice "I" (ENTER
    MRS. "I").

MRS. "I" Hello, there.

GENE SUNBURN Are you ready, players? (BOTH
    REPLY YES)   Here's your first question worth
    two points. "Which vowel is also the first letter of
    the alphabet?" (BUZZER SOUNDS) Yes, Mrs. "I"?

MRS. "I" Umm. . . "A"?

GENE SUNBURN Right. . . and you have two points.
    (APPLAUSE) The next question is worth five

points. "Which vowel makes the 'ih' sound, as in 'pig' and 'stick'? (BUZZER SOUNDS Yes, Mr. Owens?

MR. OWENS "I"!

GENE SUNBURN Right! (APPLAUSE) I'm amazed that you didn't get that one, Mrs. "I".

MRS. "I" Well, I, uh. . .

GENE SUNBURN (INTERRUPTING). . . No matter! The score is now five to two. Mr. Owens is our leader.

MR. OWENS Yea. . .

GENE SUNBURN The next question is worth three points. "Which vowel makes the 'eh' sound as in 'get', 'wet', and 'egg'? (PAUSE) No? Well, it's the letter "E". No one guessed on that one, so we double the score on the next question. For six points: "How many vowels are there?" Think hard. (BUZZER SOUNDS) Yes Mrs. "I"?

MRS. "I" Let me see, uh. . . there's "A", "E", "I", "O", "U",. . . That's five!

GENE SUNBURN Well, actually there are six.

MRS. "I" Oh. . .

GENE SUNBURN Along with "A", "E", "I", "O", and "U", "Y" is sometimes used as a vowel. However, since the main vowels are: "A", "E", "I", "O", and "U", we will accept five as an answer. (APPLAUSE) Mrs. "I" is now our leader with the score eight to five as we come to our "DOUBLE OR NOTHING" round. In this round, the person who answers the question correctly will double his or her score. But, if the answer is not correct, the contestant answering will lose everything. At the end of this round the player with the highest score will be our grand prize winner. What is the prize for today's winning player, Johnny?

JOHNNY Well, Gene, our winner today will receive five vowels a day for the rest of his or her life! (APPLUASE)

GENE SUNBURN Oh, wow. What a prize! Are you ready, contestants? (THE CONTESTANTS MAKE SOUNDS OF AGREEMENT) Fine! Now to double your score, "Which vowel makes the 'oo' sound as in 'pool' and 'school'?" (BUZZER SOUNDS) Yes, Mr. Owens?

MR. OWENS Oh,. . . um,. . . "U"!

GENE SUNBURN Well, "U" can make the "oo" sound, but in "pool" and "school" it's two "O's" put together.

MR. OWENS Ohh.

GENE SUNBURN So, the answer is "O".

MRS. "I" That means I won!

MR. OWENS Ohh no.

GENE SUNBURN I'm sorry, Mr. Owens, Mrs. "I" is our winner and champion today.

MR. OWENS Oh, no.

GENE SUNBURN (APPLAUSE) Tune in again next time when once again we'll play Guess That Vowel. Until then, this is Gene Sunburn, saying "Goodbye and good vowels."
(MUSIC AND APPLAUSE UP AND OUT)

The puppet team must carefully select its plays if it wishes to be successful. Puppeteers and script writers should be aware of the fundamentals involved in writing scripts for puppet plays. If they are familiar with these fundamentals, and creatively build around this structure, they will have in the resulting scripts a solid nucleus of success. It is then the responsibility of the puppeteer to make the puppet, and script, come alive on stage. And it is this combination which makes puppetry such a fascinating method of communication.

14

A Puppet Philosophy For Churches

Churches were among the first organizations to recognize and to capitalize on the current revival of interest in puppetry. Church leaders and lay people have incorporated puppetry into existing programs, or established new ones, and the results have been spectacular. Since training seminars were first established to properly equip beginning puppeteers in the art of puppetry, individuals from over 6,000 churches have been trained. Many of these have begun active puppet teams as part of their church's Christian education program. And where quality puppetry has been the goal, invitations for performances outside the church setting have been received.

Puppetry, of course, is unable to transform a lifeless church education program into a highly successful one all by itself. After all, puppets need human help! But the addition of puppets to a church program can stimulate new growth in the entire church. And many churches have found that the addition of puppet teams has greatly influenced the success of their educational structures. The reasons for their success are the same as those for puppet teams with other affiliations: puppets command attention and present a message at the same time they are entertaining the audience.

The organization of a puppet team in a church for the first time is a fairly simple task. There are several important considerations, however, which must be mentioned. First, the church leaders must understand that the reason for successful puppetry is found in its ability to entertain. At first glance, some church leaders may find this aspect unsuitable and at odds with their philosophy of Christian education. Puppets which entertain, however, are not necessarily in conflict with a fundamentally sound program of Christian education. Both puppet team and church staff should understand that puppets use entertainment as a means of obtaining the end result of understanding in the mind of the child. We live in a world of entertainment, through radio, television, and the other media. These media have successfully entertained and, unfortunately, presented various content lessons at the same time. Children are used to this highly visual and entertaining orientation and also respond to it in church settings. Learning does not have to be dull to be effective! Church leaders need to be aware that puppet lessons can be fun and educational.

A second philosophical consideration is closely connected to the first. Because puppets are so loveable and fun a church puppet team can become too involved in the entertainment aspect and lose sight of the major consideration, that of presenting a message. The director of the church puppet team has the responsibility to insure that the puppet team maintains the proper perspective regarding the use of puppetry as an entertaining method of presenting an inspirational message. The success of the puppet team in church ministry is directly related to the director's ability to maintain this perspective.

How does a puppet team get started in a church? Perhaps the best way is to utilize existing structures as much as possible. If the church has an active drama department, the puppet team might serve as a sub-unit since puppeteers use all the drama techniques, including lighting, props and sound effects. The director should be trained in the use of puppets as a teaching tool, hopefully at a seminar conducted by Puppet Productions. The director's responsibilities are more fully outlined in chapter 3 and a careful reading of that chapter should be made before proceeding in the establishment of a puppet ministry or to the selection of a puppet director. Also, although an existing drama club serves as a good beginning organization for a puppet team, the same adult leader should not try to direct both groups. The time required to develop the puppet team will not allow this dual capacity.

Just as the director cannot be involved in too many outside activities, individuals becoming puppeteers must also determine priorities before joining the puppet team. Some members of the youth choir are excellent candidates for puppetry since they are already disciplined to rehearsal schedules, etc. Puppetry is also an attractive opportunity for those who like to perform but cannot sing. Most puppeteers in churches will come from the more involved and dedicated young people in the church. The advantage of a quality puppet program, however, is that after a brief period of operation more young people will be in this category.

Once the director and puppeteers have been selected, work can begin in preparation for actual performances. It is important to have professional puppets available at this time. If sub-quality or toy puppets are used, enthusiasm for the project frequently wanes. There seems to be a positive correlation between the quality of the puppet and the quality of the puppeteer. The new puppet team should have the advantage of professional puppets. The puppet team should meet regularly to practice techniques, prepare and tape new scripts, make props and build stages. More frequent rehearsals are necessary until the puppeteers become proficient and are able to work well together as a team. A minimum of four puppeteers and one adult director should be available to form the puppet team.

Experience has shown that the ideal size for a puppet team is 4-5 members. Any fewer in number and the type of presentation which can be given is severely limited. Larger teams tend to become disorganized and generally do not work well. A basic rule to remember in church puppetry is that every member must have a definite responsibility. If this is not the case, puppeteers become disinterested and drop out. To maintain interest in the puppet ministry and the quality of the performance, each puppeteer must have definite assignments as well as a feeling of accomplishment.

Using puppets in the church can be done in several different ways. First, care must be taken not to over-use the puppets. Over-exposure can destroy the usefulness of puppets in church ministries. One way of avoiding over-exposure is to vary the method of presentation. Longer plays, 8-10 minutes in length, which present Bible truths should be presented no more frequently than once a month. One reason for this is that the puppet team would not have adequate rehearsal time to perform more often and still maintain professional quality. Puppet teams must remember that the entertainment aspect of their presentation is being compared with professional television. Children can be severe critics and their criticism is demonstrated in not attending the puppet production. Major puppet presentations, therefore, should be scheduled to allow enough rehearsal time.

Puppets can still be used each week, however. Select a special puppet character who will perform regularly each week. The personality of this puppet should be developed thoroughly until the children can know him, identify with him, and look forward to seeing him. The functions of this single puppet are many: he can serve as song leader, announcer, master of ceremonies, whatever the occasion calls for. This puppet should have a name and serve as an assistant teacher. If awards or decorations are given to the children, let the puppet make the presentation; it will be something the children will remember. This special puppet friend can also pass out any material to be taken home, introduce guests, deliver brief monologues, or interact with the teacher. Each week, this special puppet should vary his involvement slightly so the children will not know what he is going to say or do. Even with the variety, the puppet should perform no longer than 4-6 minutes each week. The puppet director will also need to insure that the puppet's personality (chapter 7) is consistantly performed from week to week. This will require the same puppeteer to manipulate the puppet and provide the voice. If the puppeteer is unable to attend, the puppet should not be used. A different puppet character can be introduced in his absence and an explanation ("our friend went away for the weekend") for the change should be given the children.

With these thoughts in mind, an examination can be made of the use of puppets in various ministries and programs of the church. Although there is a great deal of overlap from program to program, each area will be dealt with separately.

1.   CHILDREN'S CHURCH. The children's church program is a extremely important part of the ministry of the church. It is here that children gain not only an understanding of the basic teachings of the church, but also an introduction to the basic working of the church itself. Many churches fail to favorably impress their children because of the nature of their children's programs. Children are different from adults; they have different values, different attitudes, different attention spans, etc. And they must be treated accordingly. Children's church should not be a reflection of adult church on a smaller scale for that is the formula for boredom in the mind of the child. The effective children's church program should be able to teach God's Word in an interesting and relevant way. For children to incorporate the truth of what they are being taught, they must be motivated. And a significant factor in this motivation is whether the child enjoys the church experience. Children who are met each Sunday by unsmiling adults, determined to keep the little monsters under control for another hour, usually have a negative feeling about church. The best way for Christ's teachings to take root in these little lives, is for an adult to work with them in a program which recognizes the limits of children. Do not shut off the energy of children; channel it!

It takes more than a recognition of childhood limitations, of course, to insure a smoothly running program for children's church. Creative planning and careful scheduling also helps. The use of puppets, like all other aspects of children's church, must be well-organized. Problems in discipline in many instances can be traced to poor planning and preparation. This planning should incorporate puppets into the overall picture. If a major Bible truth presentation is to be made with the entire puppet team, the children should be prepared for what the lesson is about. Puppet shows should never be presented without adequate introduction. Teachers should prepare the class for the subject which the puppets will teach. An adequate introduction should include some discussion of the theme of the puppet show (forgiveness, self-acceptance, etc.). Then, following the puppet presentation, the adult leader should help the children understand how they can apply what has been taught into the routine of their lives. Material should be prepared which informs the parent about the lesson and suggests activities which the family can perform that reinforce the truth of the lesson.

One additional factor should be mentioned which influences not only the ability of puppets to successfully perform, but any activity when little children are present. The age span of the children must be carefully considered. It is nearly impossible to have an interesting relevant primary church program if there is a wide span of ages. Even with small groups, children should be subdivided into age groups so the lessons can be better tailored to their ability to attend and comprehend. Experience has shown that pre-schoolers should be in one group, grades 1-3 in a second group, and grades 4-6 in a third group. The establishment of smaller groups based on age may increase the work of the adult leaders but it will significantly influence the level of learning by the children.

Within each age group, activities should be structured which emphasize variety. Remember, for many children, children's church is only part of the Sunday morning schedule, they have already been sitting through a Sunday school program. Coordinating children's church activities with those of the Sunday school department makes a more smoothly running program, and one which is much more enjoyable for the children.

A sample children's church service using puppets is listed below. This schedule should only be used once a month when the large puppet play is used. It gives a model, however, for the variety, short activities and changes of pace which are needed when working with children. This schedule would be used with grades 1-3.

10:50 AM Refreshments. Punch and cookies provide a good transition between Sunday school and church. Ample time should be given.

11:05 AM Welcome. The teacher welcomes the children and recognizes any visitors. (This can be done by the "special puppet" in other weeks.) The hour's activities should be briefly noted. Prayer.

11:10 AM Special puppet. The adult leader introduces the special puppet character who leads in a sing-a-long. This is an excellent time and method to introduce and teach one new song.

11:15 AM The teacher introduces the puppet lesson and prepares the children for its content message.

11:20 AM Presentation of the Bible truth. The puppet team performs an eight minute play. These are most effectively done when the puppets present the essence of a Bible story rather than the actual story itself. In other words, situations relevant to the children can be used to present Biblical principles. These are often more readily understood by the children than the actual Bible story. A good example of how this is done can be found in the play "Short Subjects" in chapter 13, Writing Puppet Plays. This fact should be kept in mind when the scripts are being prepared.

11:28 AM The adult teacher reviews the story and makes the application for the children.

11:33 AM Activity time, musical games, etc.

11:43 AM Bible memory verse time. Select a scripture verse which relates to the puppet lesson for memorization by the children.

11:53 AM The adult leader should review the new song taught earlier by the special puppet character.

11:55 AM End this children's church session with some exciting game or activity. This will need to be an open-ended activity until the adult worship service is over.

This schedule will be modified of course, by the particular needs of each local church. Generally, however, this has been widely successful for using puppets in a children's church program.

2. SUNDAY SCHOOL. The use of puppets in the Sunday school program must be coordinated with puppet programs in other areas of the church. Puppets should not be featured in both Sunday school and children's church on the same day. If a major Bible truth presentation is being used in one hour, the "special friend" puppet should be featured in the other. Cooperation and com-

munication between adult leaders in both departments is essential.

If your particular church does not have a special children's church program, the recommendation for children's church in the previous section should be used for the Sunday school program instead. Read carefully through the section in children's church and adapt its suggestions to your existing Sunday school program.

3. VACATION BIBLE SCHOOL. With some modifications, the information on children's church is appropriate for Vacation Bible School. There is one major factor, however, that must be considered. Vacation Bible Schools often attract children that are not used to attending church and are unfamiliar, therefore, with the routine and scheduling of church programs. They are only familiar with secular programs and are used to being entertained. It is important to feature high quality puppet shows as one of the central features of Vacation Bible School. Because this program meets only for one or two weeks a year, major puppet productions can be presented several times during the week without over-exposing the puppets. The puppet team should be aware of the VBS schedule so they can prepare several shows to present. Planning ahead and perhaps scheduling some extra rehearsals will permit the team to maintain consistently high standards for all productions. On days when major Bible truths are not presented, the "special puppet" technique will want to be used. Vacation Bible School provides one of the best opportunities most churches have for exciting youngsters about attending church. Unfortunately, most churches fail to properly use VBS for this purpose. The church that utilizes

puppetry in its Vacation Bible School will be gratified by the results.

4.   BACKYARD BIBLE CLUBS. Backyard Bible Clubs can take two different forms: the first serves the same function as a Vacation Bible School only it is conducted in a private home. This type generally meets on a continuing basis, once a week. The different time involved with each program requires a slightly different schedule and approach with puppets.

a.   Backyard Bible Clubs that meet every day for one week are most similar to the format presented for Vacation Bible School. Puppets can be used more frequently, if the puppet team is prepared, without danger of the children becoming tired of them. As is the case with other activities involving children, variety and changes of pace are necessary. In addition, it is often useful to create a festive, carnival atmosphere to help attract children in the neighborhood. Balloons and candy might be a wise investment. Backyard Bible Clubs should not be allowed to drag out in time. The program should be brief, feature a lot of variety such as songs, games, puppet show, refreshments, stories and announcements. When the children leave, make sure they want to come back for more the next day. Perhaps the "Special Puppet" friend can supervise a project or contest to build interest throughout the week.

b.   Weekly meetings. The Bible Clubs that meet weekly are more similar to Sunday schools and should follow a similar program. The major difference is that children will attend that might not be from church families. These children, and church-oriented children as well, deserve the best and innovative program which the imagination of church leaders can devise. Puppets will play a major role in these creative methods of church outreach and education.

5.   BUILDING BUS ROUTES Developing bus routes is becoming an increasingly used method by churches seeking to serve more people. This involves the church buses following pre-selected routes to pick up children interested in attending Sunday school. The church with an active puppet team can use puppets to develop interest in the new bus routes.

Once plans have been made to begin the new route, the puppet team should start to perform front yard puppet plays in the area. Colorful flyers should be distributed announcing the time, date, and address of each show. A performance should be scheduled for each 70-80 homes on the route. The puppet team will need to coordinate with the bus route director to see what dates are desired and the bus will need to be driven into the neighborhood when the puppet shows are performed so the children can see it. The puppet shows should be on the Saturday before the bus route begins.

On Saturday morning approximately 30 minutes before show time, the same team which distributed flyers for the puppet show should return to the neighborhood passing out balloons. This will create interest and help gather a crowd at the puppet stage location. Festive music should be played for 5 or 10 minutes. No serious themes should be presented at this time since it is difficult to control children at an outdoor performance and serious presentations are not as easy for non-church children to watch. The puppets should present a good quality, fun, entertaining show. The puppet team must have an adequate sound system. A guitar amplifier-speaker is adequate and microphones should be used by the host. An adult leader, puppeteer, or supporting youth worker can then talk to the children and inform them that the puppets can be seen the next day at church and that the bus will come through the neighborhood to pick them up. Be sure to specify the time. If the puppet team has done a good job, and plans have been well-executed, the children will want to come the next day to see their puppet friends again.

6. SHOPPING CENTERS and PARKS. Churches frequently lose sight of the fact that they are supposed to go into the world with their message. They expect the people to come to them. The use of puppets presents a natural vehicle for the church to make itself known where the people are. Shopping centers welcome puppet teams which are of good quality because it is an additional attraction for their stores — another reason for shoppers to patronize their businesses. Departments of Park and Recreation are also receptive to having puppet teams perform.

The church puppet team, then, has popular areas in which it can perform. What kind of plays should it present? The puppet team must remember that outside performances are not ideal circumstances to perform serious presentations. The situation does not allow as much discipline as is generally desired and there is often other noise and distractions competing for attention. For these reasons, shows should be devoted to entertaining the audience and, as was the case in Building Bus Routes," invitations should be extended after (or during) the show to attend the church or Sunday school and see more of the puppets.

Puppets appeal especially to children. And parents notice when people make an attempt to make their children happy. It is good public relations for the church puppet teams to perform in shopping centers and parks; it shows parents that churches are concerned about children and families. The puppet team should recognize the tremendous potential in this area and channel some of its energy into developing this area of ministry. The results are well worth the effort required.

Puppets are fun! They are a novel way not only of providing entertainment, but of giving instruction as well. In the last several years, countless churches have discovered this fact and have seen a resurgence in their youth and Christian education programs. Puppets cannot do everything, but they do provide an important element in the formula for success — a success that is achieved with hard work, planning, organization, and yes, an enjoyable time. Whether used in a church with a large puppet team, or a single puppeteer, puppets work!

15

A Puppet Philosophy For Schools

Recently, educators have begun to recognize the tremendous usefulness that puppets can have in schools if they are used correctly and with a definite purpose. Traditionally, puppets have been seen not as teachers but only as entertainers or "things made from old socks during craft time." Slowly, however, a dramatic change has taken place in the thinking of many teachers and administrators. Puppets can teach and they can be an integral part of many instructional programs.

The reasons for the success of puppets in the classroom have been discussed before: they have the ability to command attention; they help increase concentration in the subject matter presented; they motivate students to perform well. These are factors which are of significant importance when puppets are used as instructional tools and are integrated into a total learning experience. So, Puppet Productions has developed, tested, and refined a total package of instructional puppetry that has proven dramatically successful in public school use. This package benefits from the novelty of the puppets themselves, and from their ability to command attention, but it also adds several important ingredients in its formula for success.

School puppet teams, like those of any other affiliation, are centered around the director — who must take an active role in all aspects of the program. For instructional puppetry, a teacher usually fills this position. In elementary schools, the teacher/director is generally from the 5th or 6th grade classes, since this allows closer contact with the puppeteers. Puppeteers are chosen from the students in the upper grades, primarily from the 5th and 6th. This then, is the composition of the puppet team: a teacher/director and students/puppeteers. The use of students as

The key to the use of puppets in schools is allowing students to form the puppet teams. These elementary youngsters are helping teach their classmates.

puppeteers is an important part of instructional
puppetry. Their enthusiasm for puppetry greatly aids
their ability to perform high-quality shows. The instructional puppet team maintains a regular schedule of
rehearsals and must become accomplished in its
puppetry before attempting any actual performances.
Many directors of instructional puppet teams have
found it useful to hold auditions at the end of each year
so successful candidates can practice during the
summer and shorten the amount of time spent on
preparation in the fall. Frequently, the parents of
children selected for the puppet team are willing to
invest in a personal puppet for their puppeteer so
rehearsing does not prove a problem during summer
vacation.

Once school starts in the fall, the puppet team will
need to spend additional time after regular school
hours perfecting their teamwork under the watchful eye
of the director. Important factors to consider at this
time, and some techniques to make rehearsals better,
are listed in chapter 4. In addition to working on their
puppetry, team members must also become familiar
with the sound system, stage, and lighting if it is desired.
Further, the puppeteer must be thoroughly familiar with
the scripts they will use to teach various subjects to their
classmates. Ideally, much of the script material will be
memorized to insure better lip sync with the puppets.

The director and puppeteers have been selected,
trained, and are now ready for actual performances.
What next? The program of instructional puppetry
developed by Puppet Productions uses puppet plays to
complement the in-class activities that are administered
by the teacher. The first order of business, therefore, is
to schedule performances in the various classrooms at
each school. The teacher is contacted, a date and time
established, and plans are made for the puppet show.

the script, lists of suggested learning activities to follow the show, and new vocabulary words, should also be sent. If, for example, the scheduled lesson is on metrics, with emphasis on liquid measurement, a list of vocabulary words might include liter, deciliter, dekaliter, etc. If the puppet script contains any new and un- familiar words, the teacher should be advised so she can take appropriate steps *before* the puppet team arrives. Otherwise, the students will not thoroughly understand the lesson and their attention may wander.

The puppet team should have lessons available to them, with which they are familiar, which are suitable for the grade levels in the school. Elementary puppet teams should be capable of performing appropriate presentations to either kindergarten or 6th grade students. All grade levels are captivated by quality instructional puppet shows. This cross-aged instruction serves a very valuable function: not only are the student puppeteers helping teach those in the audience, but their familiarity with the lesson, and their constant repetition by performing it, also reinforces their own understanding of the particular concept. The student puppeteers will discover what teachers have known for years: you learn more when you prepare to teach! The puppeteers will themselves become major beneficiaries of an instructional puppetry program

This, then, is the essence of the instructional puppet program: students teaching students through the use of puppets. This formula is successful primarily because it gains and maintains the attention of the students. Why? Because instructional puppetry is not simply a relating of basic educational subjects to the student. It is fun! A quality puppet show is highly entertaining at the same time it presents its message. And because of this entertainment aspect, children concentrate more with puppet lessons than they do when the teacher simply presents the material. The puppets are excellent models for acceptable behavior and, as they become familiar with the students, many children will identify with the various personalities presented. (See chapter 7.)

Modern society has become increasingly dependent on listening skills in everyday interaction. Where reading and writing once held the unquestioned position of necessary skills, the listening skills have become steadily more important. This is the result of a society which has become oriented toward radio and television, and away from the written media. Instructional puppetry recognizes this development and builds upon it. With the children giving their undivided attention to the puppet show, they are actively involved in *listening* to what is being said. They are learning *how to listen,* a very important need in today's world.

The innovative teacher will utilize this ability of puppets to the fullest extent. Following the show, activities can be planned which reinforce the need for active listening. Several students, for example can be chosen at random to reenact the play, complete with dialog and mannerisms. They should try to duplicate their puppet counterparts. This is a fun exercise and one which teaches the students the value of listening carefully to what is being said by others.

Another exercise to show how effectively the students have heard, and understood, the lesson, is to ask questions based on the play itself. This technique has been used with visual learning (reading) for many years. It remains, in fact, a mainstay of the verbal section in most standardized tests. ("First read the paragraph, then answer the questions based on the information you have read.") Questions following a

puppet show should find their answers in the content of
the performance.

Having upper grade students perform as puppeteers
also provides another significant advantage: students in
the lower grades realize that they, too, can become
puppeteers if they learn well. This provides additional
motivation for some students who would like to be on
the team. Obviously, this is not an important factor for
kindergarten students — the reward is too far away to
be meaningful. But the influence of this motivating
factor increases as the students get closer to the time
when they can be considered for puppeteers.

After the puppet team has performed each play
several times and become thoroughly familiar with
them, additional materials will need to be developed.
The children are often the best source for new scripts as

Zachery Daiquri is the defendent in "Alcohol on Trial" an
educational lesson on the effects of alcohol on the human body.
Puppets representing the human heart, brain, stomach and liver
serve as witnesses in the trial.

they become more involved in all of the aspects of puppetry. Using the guidelines established, the puppet director should encourage puppeteers — and any students — to express themselves creatively by writing new scripts for puppet production. This is an excellent outlet for the more creative students who can express themselves in writing. And, since the puppet plays focus on one specific aspect of elementary education, the process of script writing also involves reinforcing previously learned lesson areas. A better and more highly educated student is the result. The puppet director who works closely with the team, encouraging it to do more, will find an educational bonanza in puppets. In so doing, both teacher and student will discover that learning can be fun. The concerned educator should recognize the visual orientation of today's communication systems, comprehend the entertainment aspects of this medium, and incorporate the advantages of it into an instructional program which uses puppets.

School puppet teams should be aware that they will be asked to perform in many different settings in addition to the classroom. The innovative approach of instructional puppetry makes the puppet team an ideal target for invitations from various outside groups. Service clubs, civic organizations, PTAs, even the Board of Education may request a performance from the puppet team. This is extremely beneficial for the entire school system since it allows the taxpayers to witness how the basics of education have been coupled with innovative methods to produce quality education for their children. Many school districts with public relations problems wish they could buy the type of favorable publicity generated from school puppet teams performing in the community as well as at school.

Many concerned educators and students of human behavior have become increasingly aware of the role which the parents and family play in the child's education. Recognizing that the school cannot accomplish their task by themselves, programs have been initiated which attempt to enlist the cooperation of parents. Puppets are an excellent source of program material for such endeavors. Many parents do not realize the complex factors which influence education. They are not aware of the roles they play simply by being models of behavior for their children. Parents who *need* to be reached by the schools are often the very ones who throw away school bulletins, do not attend parent conferences, or ignore (and resent) "advice" given by the teacher, principal or counselor. A cleverly written and performed puppet play, however, can both entertain and inform these parents.

A model puppet family can act out the evening routine of many families. This should be subtle in its approach. Behavior which is harmful to the education of the child, such as no verbal interaction between parent and child, should be exaggerated to the point that the members of the audience can examine themselves to see if they do the same things. Low-key commentary can follow the show. Shows highlighting the positive factors of parental involvement should also be developed. One such show might demonstrate how the father who enjoys reading, and who reads at home while his children are around, will be a model for his children — and they will likely find reading a more enjoyable experience as a result. In other words, instructional puppetry can become a program of total education, educating and developing the abilities of parents as well as children. This side product of puppetry in the schools cannot be valued in terms of money. The use of puppets in schools is limited only by the imagination, energy, and amount of time available for puppet-related activity by the director and team.

Puppets can also be used by insightful teachers for uses outside the strict definition of teaching. One such use allows the careful observer to gain glimpses into the students' self-concepts and identities. This is done by allowing each student to select one particular puppet from among several different types. Experience has shown that most students select puppets which are similar to them in personality, dress, coloring or cultural and ethnic background. Even when animals are selected there is usually some similarity of trait reflected. These subtle observations can be quite useful to the good teacher. How? If the teacher is more fully aware of the feelings, attitudes, motivations, etc., of the student, he or she can create a learning environment which is suitable for that individual student. And it is in this type of atmosphere that effective learning can best take place. Self-concepts, hopes, dreams, learning styles, even ambitions are observed when people pick the "puppet of their choice." The educated eye sees much more because it is actively *watching* not just *seeing*. Body language has been studied for years by experts in communication; perhaps puppetry will give birth to a new vehicle of communication: puppet language.

Instructional puppetry can also be adapted to the traditional classroom exercises like Reader's Theatre. Reader's Theatre is another way of helping students learn to read by increasing their motivation and interest in reading. Reader's Theatre is similar to many other types of oral interpretation, but the students are involved in several different ways.

The materials necessary include: an interesting story from a book, puppets, students and a few chairs or stools. First, select a good story, one student and puppet for each character in the story, a stool for each student, a copy of the story or script for each participating student, and a narrator. You are now ready to begin rehearsal; no scenery or costumes are needed because action is only suggested and must be visualized by the audience. The narrator establishes the setting and provides continuity and sequence.

Some preparation is necessary before the actual performance. This preparation includes: selection or creation of the story, adaptation of material, taping the script, interpreting the author's ideas, and reconstructing the meaning of the author. The involvement of the students in these activities causes the technique to become a powerful instructional tool which greatly enhances the learning process. Reader's Theatre becomes an active, not a passive, instructional tool.

Reader's Theatre is a simple activity with multiple

This teacher, and her class, have discovered that learning can be more fun when lessons are occasionally presented by puppets.

rewards. There is a reason for reading, a process and purpose in rereading in rehearsal, and a striving for excellence in the preparation and production of the tape to be used with the puppets. In rehearsal, the readers simply sit on stools, read the story, and "become" the specific characters of the story. The narrator reads the linking parts of the story. The "he saids" and "Mary screamed" portions are omitted. The readers interpret the story with voice, expressions and body movement. The readers face the audience only when they are actually speaking.

Ready to begin?

— Select a familiar story that the readers like – one that tells a good story with a lot of conversation and interaction.

— Decide who will read the various "parts" or characters in the story.

— All readers sit with their backs to the audience except when they are reading their "part."

— Select a narrator; two in some cases.

— As soon as the readers know the words, tape it for use with the puppets or try it out on an audience and then tape it.

— Practice working with the puppets and the tape.

— After one "team" masters the concept, use the puppets, tape and scripts to teach the idea to the rest of the students, another class, a group of teachers, aides or parents.

— Keep adding stories to your repertoire.

— Use the puppets either to introduce the idea, to give the finished presentation — or anywhere in between.

— Encourage students to write and direct their own stories and scripts.

This is only the beginning. Let the students try

their own ideas as you guide their efforts with positive support, acceptance and enthusiasm.

Your Puppetry Reader's Theatre will stimulate creative imagination, improve reading through creating a desire to read, enhance literary appreciation, encourage "reluctant readers" to participate, increase comprehension skills in both listening and reading, plus motivate writing and a need for "knowing how" to communicate an idea.

Puppets can also be used with any number of ideas which come with teaching experience. The more experience a teacher has, the more he will be able to adapt puppets into the classroom activities. For new teachers, however, and to show some examples of how puppets can be used, the following list of "trydeas" (try and idea) is given. This is just a suggested list for a start and should be added to, to meet individual classroom needs and abilities.

A puppet can be used as a special guest teacher, as shown in this picture. The guest teacher is a frequent visitor to the classroom and his appearances are greeted with enthusiasm.

1. Have a "Nursery Rhyme Round-Up." The puppets can come on stage and say a nursery rhyme and then have the children repeat it with them. As a related craft, the children can construct props to help act out the nursery rhyme, such as a lamb for Mary, a shoe for the old woman. (grades K-3)

2. Provide time after a presentation for the students to interact with the puppets. Let them ask questions about the lesson, themselves, or whatever. This is an excellent method to help the teacher understand the thinking processes of her students. (grades K-6)

3. Write individual or class notes to the puppet team, inviting them to teach a particular lesson, song, poem, or other appropriate activity. Follow up the performance by having the class write "thank you" notes. (grades 1-3)

4. Puppet teams should have special programs for major holidays, Thanksgiving for example. Before the puppets perform, have the children tell, tape, or write a story about the first Thanksgiving. Then, after watching the puppet show have them repeat the exercise and see how much they have learned. (grades 1-3)

5. Before the puppet team gives its presentation, tell the class that some children will be chosen to reenact the play when the puppets are finished. Good listeners should be able to remember the story and many of its major points. This exercise fosters active listeners. (grades K-6)

6. Puppets provide an excellent vehicle for children to respond without fear to particular "imaginary" situations. The student is given a puppet and the teacher creates a set of circumstances to which the puppet (puppeteer) must respond. For example:

"The puppet is seated on a bench and has completed his lunch except for his favorite pie, which he has deliberately saved for last. A bully comes along and takes away the pie. What will the puppet say or do?" The child then speaks through the puppet and the teacher can gain valuable insight into the child's problem-solving abilities, self-concept, etc. One observation to come from this activity has been made by speech therapists who have discovered that some students speaking through the puppets have done so without verbal handicaps (such as stuttering) that affect their own speech. For these children, being able to temporarily assume the personality of a neutral puppet is good therapy. (grades K-6)

7. Have a talk show format using puppets as a master of ceremonies and several guests. The M.C. can introduce the person with questions and find out more about the guest. The boys and girls using the puppets as guests can play either themselves or someone they admire. (grades 4-6)

8. Using a lion puppet, develop a program called "What's My Lion?" The lion plays the part of the moderator and a puppet is used as the challenging counterpart. The class then asks questions about the puppet's occupation. This may require some research about the particular job — and it helps the student learn the value of the library and resource books. Other game show formats can also be modified for classroom use. (grades 4-6)

9. Puppets may dramatize the beginning of an "unfinished story" and ask the pupils to tell or write how they think the story would end. This is an excellent exercise for creative thinking. Was it the lady, or the tiger? (grades 4-6)

Educators have just "scratched the surface" of the potential value in using puppets as instructional tools. But they have made an exciting beginning. Puppets have proven themselves to be valuable tools for communicating lesson content in a stimulating and entertaining way. The innovative teacher will recognize their worth as an important factor in an overall program for education, and will incorporate puppetry into his or her program. At a time when education increasingly appears to be a struggle, the fun of puppetry will be a welcome relief.

16

Puppets As Entertainers

Puppets are capable of performing in many different capacities: they can be teachers, preachers, friends — the list is endless. But one common denominator present in all the puppet roles is the ability of the puppet to entertain. The success of puppet teams to captivate their audiences is found in their ability to blend the content of the show with a professional-quality and entertaining puppet show. *Puppets must entertain.*

Determining *how* a puppet will entertain is limited only by the creativity of the puppeteer, director, and script writers. How do human entertainers relate to their audiences? With humor, music, drama? Puppets can entertain in the same way.

Humor is one of the best forms of puppet entertainment since it capitalizes on the novelty of puppets to create a favorable impression with the audience. And humor can be written into nearly every puppet script, even into serious plays, without adversely effecting the content. Experience will be a key factor in determining the form and amount of humor which you will want to use. A note of caution must be reemphasized at this point. When performing live, the puppet team must be disciplined enough that it doesn't become so carried away with extemporaneous humor that the main thrust of the performance is lost. The director will need to provide guidance for his puppeteers in helping them develop their creativity for ad-lib humor without distracting from the performance of the overall team. There may be occasions when a puppeteer will have to be corrected if the ad-lib comments do not add to the quality of the performance. The director must make this determination.

Perhaps the most frequent and useful method of having puppets act strictly as entertainers is when using them as musicians. New musical numbers can be written especially for the puppets or, better yet, use puppets to perform famous songs of "star" performers. An Afro human hand and arm puppet, for example, is an instant hit when playing the trumpet and singing to the sound track of Louis Armstrong. When imitating star performers, make sure you copy the mannerisms or personality traits which the individual may have. Louis Armstrong, for example, would not be complete without a white handkerchief mopping his brow partway through the performance. The closer the characterization is to reality, the better it will be received by the audience. Musical numbers can be performed by soloists, soloists with backup, groups, or as a complete musical with cast. Some excellent musical numbers which have been successfully performed by puppets are listed below. These numbers include those with church-orientations as well as those with strictly entertainment emphasis.

1. THE LAUGHING SONG — a very amusing song which basically consists of a laugh track. This should be performed by a human hand and arm puppet. From the record *Everything's All Right.* Canaan Records, CAS9697.

2. . . .AND THAT'S THE TRUTH — a seventeen-minute children's musical with church emphasis. Ideal for combination performance with puppets and children's choirs. Light Records, LS5659.

3   CHARLIE THE HAMSTER SINGS BIBLE STORIES — twelve numbers with country western flavor, ideal for three rod-arm and one human hand and arm puppet. Singcord from Zondervan, ZLP929.

4. FREE TO BE YOU AND ME — an immaginative album by Marlo Thomas which stresses the individuality of children. Bell Records, 1110.

5. THE BEST OF THE MIGHTY CLOUDS OF JOY — informal gospel sounds for performance by a quartet of Afro puppets. Peacock, PLP-183.

6. WALKIN' IN GOD'S COUNTRY — for gospel quartets. Light Records, LS-5525.

7. WALKIN' IN THIS WORLD — for gospel quartets. Supreme, S-218.

8. ZACH, JR. — a children's musical which can be done entirely with puppets or in combination with a children's choir. Light Records, LS5620.

The following six albums are by Andre Crouch and the Disciples and are excellent sound tracks for performances with Afro puppets.

9. TAKE THE MESSAGE EVERYWHERE — Light 5504.

10. KEEP ON SINGIN' — Light, 5546.

11. SOULFULLY — Light, 5581.

12. JUST ANDRE — Light, 5596.
13. LIVE AT CARNEGIE HALL — Light, 5602.
14. TAKE ME BACK — Light, 5637.
15. I LIKE THE SOUND OF AMERICA — a children's musical with a patriotic theme. Light Records.
16. COOL IN THE FURNACE — a semi-sacred children's musical. Word Records.
17. THE BOY WHO CAUGHT THE FISH — the story of one little boy's encounter with Jesus. Light Records, LS5588.
18. SAM — an up-tempo folk musical dealing with respect for others as dramatized in the story of the Good Samaritan. Light Records, LS5617.
19. I WANT YOU — another excellent vehicle for combining puppets with choirs. Light Records, LS5653.
20. HEY, GOD, LISTEN — a strikingly different musical reflecting the direct, beautiful, and often naive, way children talk to God. Impact, R3237.
21. I'M SOMETHING SPECIAL — contains several numbers which are ideal for any group, despite the basic church-related theme. Singcord, ZLP 922S.
22. WHAT A WONDERFUL THING IS ME! — excellent for use with pre-schoolers. Disneyland Records, 1349.
23. JONAH'S TALE OF A WHALE — enjoyable music for any audience. Broadman Records, 4585-17.
24. CHRISTMAS WITH THE CHIPMUNKS — excellent for use with cartoon character or animal puppets. Liberty Records, LST7334.
25. SUNSHINE AND SNOWFLAKES — seasonal numbers for Christmas. Word Records, LS5625.
26. HAPPINESS IS. . . SINGING WITH MARCY — good sing-a-long music for pre-schoolers, performed with girl puppet. Singcord, ZLP862.

27. ORIGINAL RECORD CAST SESAME STREET
    — contains two numbers which are well-suited for
    puppets: "Green," teaching self-confidence and
    self-acceptance, and "Rubber Duckie," a purely
    fun song. Columbia Children's Record Library.
28. TREASURY — good Louis Armstrong numbers
    for an Afro human hand and arm puppet. MCA
    Coral, CB20027.

This is by no means an exhaustive list of musical
numbers, it is simply a brief listing of albums which have
been successfully used with puppets. You will want to
add to this list as your puppet team becomes more
involved in puppet productions which emphasizes the
entertainment aspects of puppetry. Such productions
are ideally suited for presentations before PTAs, civic
or service clubs, in shopping malls, in free park
concerts, etc. When using puppets as entertainers, just
as in their use as teachers or preachers, make sure that
adequate rehearsal time has been given to insure a
professional quality performance. You and your
audience will be delighted by the results.

17

Puppets On Television

The novelty of a puppet show has an appeal all its own. This, coupled with an energetic puppet team which insists on quality performances, forms a combination difficult to resist. Performing on television should be the goal of every puppet team, whether the main purpose of the group is educational, church-related, or strictly entertainment. And with a quality product to present, puppet teams from all these areas will find a friendly reception from television stations. A closer look at each area shows their value for television productions.

1. Educational. Puppet teams which specialize in instructional puppet shows can take advantage of both commercial stations and those affiliated with the Corporation for Public Broadcasting. The Public Broadcasting System should not be overlooked, since it numbers approximately 300

stations which specialize in educational and
cultural programming. These stations usually have
broadcasting time available for locally-produced
programs, and instructional puppet teams are
ideally suited for this task. Even though the Public
Broadcasting System stations are probably the best
source of available broadcast time for instructional
puppetry, the educationally-oriented puppet team
should not neglect the commercial stations. These
stations *must* allocate a specific amount of broadcast time to public service programming. Stations
must use this time for programs which serve the
public interest. Often this is done through inter-
views with community leaders, news specials, local
interest and cultural activities. This programming is
generally taped live with little, if any, planning or
rehearsal. Accordingly, the quality of public service
programs is often below that of commercial
programs and this is reflected in the smaller
number of viewers watching.

But public service programming does not have
to be dull or inferior in technical quality. The
puppet team which has sought excellence in its
productions and rehearsals can with little difficulty
bring that same excellence to television performances. There will always be room for quality
puppetry with instructional emphasis, whether on
a Public Broadcasting or commercial station.

2.   Church. Puppet teams whose primary orientation
      is with productions of a religious nature do not
      have the same television opportunities which exist
      for instructional teams. Public Broadcasting
      System stations are forbidden by law from airing
      programs of a religious nature. Most church
      puppet teams, however, have repertoires which

include musical numbers or skits which are strictly entertainment. Such programming would be acceptable for brief Public Broadcasting appearances.

Many churches already have some sort of television programming, whether on a regularly-scheduled or special basis. The puppet team which represents one of these churches will be able to greatly assist the content of the broadcast. Live church services, for example, usually appeal to adults, but not children. The puppet team could become a regular part of the televised service which would appeal to the children in the viewing audience. Brief puppet performances could be done live or be pre-recorded but should always be done in a separate room. An ideal spot for the puppet sequence is when announcements are being made or when the offering is taken. Having a brief puppet show at this time allows the church to conduct internal business during the televised service, without involving the television audience. Puppets also serve as an excellent outreach tool when used in this manner. After watching the puppets perform on television and attaining "celebrity" status, children respond to invitations to "come and see the puppet friends in person."

But traditional church services are not the only vehicle for television performances by puppet teams. New and highly innovative programming has been initiated by some churchmen who have recognized the role of television in modern society. Much of this new programming is aimed at younger audiences — and puppets do exceptionally well in these shows. Further, church puppet teams can utilize some of their Biblically-based plays to present lessons on the interpersonal truth of the Bible story. Zacchaeus, for example, was a Biblical figure who cheated others but was forgiven by Christ. While forgiveness is the main theme of the story, Zacchaeus' status and self concept were also important factors which can be mentioned.

An excellent puppet show can be written to stress many of the less noticed but very important truths taught by the Bible. Church puppet teams should be able to relate their performances on as many levels as possible in order to extend the influence of their ministries. Church teams, like their instructional counterparts, should have no difficulty obtaining invitations for television as long as they have superior performance standards.

3. Entertainment. Some puppet teams may be formed by individuals with no connections to either churches or schools. These teams will probably emphasize the entertainment aspect of puppetry. Time is often made available for these teams by both commercial stations with public service time, and by Public Broadcasting stations. The most important element involved in being selected for television performances is quality puppetry. Those who work hard will be afforded the opportunity to perform on television.

There are some fundamental rules for television which should be followed by every puppet team. Awareness by both director and puppeteers will greatly assist the puppet team in giving high quality shows. Puppet teams will want to add additional rules to the list as they gain experience in television performances.

1. The audio track should be pre-recorded, regardless of the length of the show. Poor quality audio is a common failure of televised puppetry — it is very distracting for the audience. Poor quality sound seriously disrupts any puppet performance,

but, in televised shows, the effect of inferior audio is even more pronounced.

2. Although most puppet groups prefer the convenience of cassette tapes, television stations prefer reel-to-reel pre-recorded tape. Record at 7½ IPS. On this point, as in other areas where cooperation between the puppet team and television station is required, the puppet director should ask about the technical requirements or preferences of the station in advance of the scheduled taping. Good public relations in this area is valuable when establishing a long-term relationship.

3. The public has come to demand higher quality performances from television entertainers. For this reason, lip sync must be thoroughly rehearsed to achieve absolute accuracy.

4. In order to accomplish accurate lip sync, the puppeteer must know the exact timing of the script. The time lag between sentences or musical numbers varies with each play and the puppeteer must not guess at the intervals; he must know the timing well enough to enter exactly where he is supposed to.

5. It is important to have the cameras record the lip sync at the beginning of each segment. This allows the viewers to begin each sentence watching the puppet's mouth, adding both to the realism and the believability for lip sync later in the sentence or musical number.

6. If for any reason the puppeteers cannot accurately begin their lip sync with the first word in the sentence, the cameras should not be focused on the puppet's mouth. Instead, have the director focus on a close-up of props, costumes, hand

Puppeteers can perform without a stage if the show is being filmed or videotaped. In this drawing the camera captures only the action of the puppets, cropping out the puppeteers.

action, etc. Then, after the dialog has started, the camera should slowly pull back until the puppet is in full view.

7.   It is not always necessary to have an elaborate stage for television productions. A single curtain stage is usually sufficient. Additional stages can be created out of pianos, risers, or props. Cameras make excellent stages for television. Simply instruct the cameraman to crop the puppeteers out of the picture. For television productions, stages sometimes are not necessary if the cameraman and director are skilled and the puppeteers do not bounce up into the picture. Operating with no stage, or partially concealing stages, can often help add realism to the production. The main consideration here is to show the puppet without revealing the puppeteer.

8.   Studio lighting is extremely important. The puppet director must inform the lighting crew about the different colored puppets scheduled for use. It is extremely difficult for contrasting colored puppets to maintain accurate color during the same scene. Light colors will wash out if too much light is used, while darker puppets tend to absorb light and require more light than usual.

9.   If the television station has the time, equipment and technical experience, it is desirable to tape the program in brief segments and then edit them into the final format. This allows for more orderly changes in sets, props and puppets. Frequently, however, it is not possible to tape the production in segments. When this is the case, the entire production will need to be taped without stopping. The puppet team will need to be thoroughly rehearsed and organized to perform the show without breaks.

10. Remember a cardinal rule for puppet performances: shows should be brief and feature quick
changes of pace. Accordingly, musical numbers
should be no longer than two to three minutes and
skits should never exceed six minutes in length.

11. REHEARSE THE SHOW UNTIL EVERY DETAIL
OF THE PERFORMANCE IS AS PERFECT AS
POSSIBLE.

Television is *the* communications tool of this age.
Puppet teams, which specialize in communications,
should take advantage of this tool and make television
performances a goal. This will serve to stimulate interest
in the puppet group and it will be a motivating factor
when striving for professional excellence.

18

Stages

Good puppetry comes in stages! This refers to more than just the development of puppeteer abilities. The nature of puppetry requires some type of stage to block the audience's view of the puppeteers during the performance. Several types of stage have been developed for use with puppets, and several objects which are not stages can be used as such if the need arises, or if some special effect is desired. Stages differ in cost and versatility, and the stage ultimately selected for use by your puppet group should be tailored to your individual requirements. Many groups will feel the need for more than one stage.

1. The curtain stage is one of the best looking portable stages. It is also relatively simple to construct. The curtain stage consists of a fabric curtain hung on sturdy plastic water pipes. The pipe must be strong enough not to sag when the

Both rod arm and human hand puppets can be used behind a simple desk "stage" if the puppeteer is skilled enough. These pictures show how additional props hide view of the puppeteer's arm.

curtain is hung. Schedule 80 PVC pipe, 1½ inches in diameter, is recommended for this purpose. Black pipe also works better than white. In addition to the lengths of pipe, several connecting fittings are also required. Thin wall, or Schedule 40, fittings for 1½ inch pipe work well. The connectors will fit snugly and do not have to be cemented. This leaves the stage easily disassembled and highly portable.

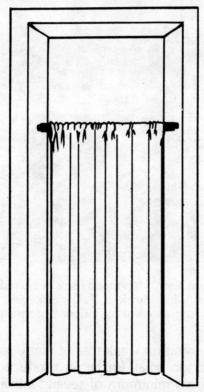

Any doorway can be converted to a puppet stage by hanging a curtain from a tension rod. The curtain must touch the floor and should be dark enough so that the puppeteers cannot be seen through it.

These puppeteers and their puppets use a two-tiered curtain stage suspended over a framework of PVC plastic pipe. This stage is highly portable and excellent for indoor performances.

One common weakness of many stages is that they are too small for larger productions. Stages should be a minimum of seven feet wide; if more than four puppets perform at once, a nine foot stage is recommended. The following materials are required.

Quanity	Description	Size	Length
1	Plastic Pipe	1½"	5'
4	Plastic Pipe	1½"	4½'
2	Plastic Pipe	1½"	2'
2	"T" Thin wall	1½"	
2	45 Elbow-Thin wall	1½"	
2	90 Elbow Thin wall	1½"	
4	Cast iron or plastic flange		
4	1" Wooden base	10" sq.	
1	Fabric curtain (Used crushed or regular velvet curtain fabric. Regular velvet will require a lining.)		15'

The plastic pipe used in this stage can be purchased at any good irrigation or landscaping supply store. The curtain stage is good-looking, functional, and easy to transport. It is not suited, however, to use outdoors since even slight breezes will cause the curtain to flap.

2. The three-tiered curtain stage allows the puppet team to have two performing levels plus a matching backdrop. This stage allows simultaneous, two-level action, such as a narrator puppet speaking from one level while action occurs on the other. Puppeteers on the lower level must perform from the kneeling position, while those at the second tier can stand. This stage is extremely attractive and has the added advantage that both sides are completely draped with curtain, thus blocking the audience view of puppeteers or

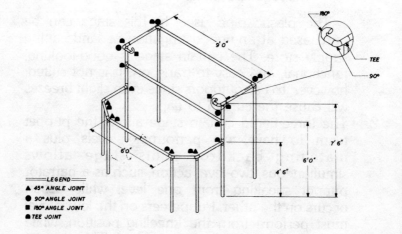

The three-tiered curtain stage described in this chapter hangs on a skeleton or PVC plastic pipe. This diagram shows the correct position for each section of pipe.

accessories backstage. The three-level curtain
stage is illustrated in drawing B and the breakdown
of required components is listed below.

Quantity	Description	Size	Length
2	Plastic Pipe	1½"	9'
2	Plastic Pipe	1½"	7½'
1	Plastic Pipe	1½"	6'
6	Plastic Pipe	1½"	4½'
2	Plastic Pipe	1½"	3'
2	Plastic Pipe	1½"	2½'
6	Plastic Pipe	1½"	1½'
4	45 Elbow-Thin wall	1½"	
2	180 Elbow-Thin wall	1½"	
12	"T" Thin wall	1½"	
8	1" Wooden bases	10" sq.	
1	Curtain (backdrop)	15x2½'	
1	Curtain (second tier)	15x2'	
1	Curtain (front)	21x4½'	
2	Curtains (sides)	4½x7½'	
2	Curtains (columns)	3'x3½'	

Some of the smaller pipe lengths may need to
be trimmed to eliminate length added to the elbow
connectors. Refer to the illustration and key for
assembly instructions.

This stage, like the single-tiered curtain stage, is
not well-suited to outdoor use. The height of both
stages may be altered if necessary, depending on
the heights of the puppeteers. If the puppeteers
are younger than college age, it may be necessary

to shorten the pipe stands on the first tier so that the puppeteers' heads do not appear above the stage when they are in the kneeling position. Make sure that this measurement is made with the use of any rubber knee pads which might be used by the puppeteers. The stage height should average the heights represented by the puppeteers. Puppeteers who are smaller can use additional kneeling pads to build up their height. Taller puppeteers will have to keep a lower profile to avoid being seen by the audience. The director should keep close tabs on this aspect of the puppet production; "can heads be seen from the back of the audience?" If so, corrective steps must be taken immediately.

The second and third levels should be shortened accordingly if this is done. The curtain for both stages should hang with one or two inches on the floor; a curtain which is too short will reveal some of the backstage activities and distract from the puppet performance. The curtain itself should not be hemmed until after it has been hung once to insure that it is long enough.

The top hem of the curtain must be six inches wide in order for it to slip easily over the pipe and fittings. Five-inch openings should also be left where "T" fittings are used to connect crosspieces to the pipe stands.

3. A simply constructed stage made from wooden paneling is ideal for both indoor and outdoor use. The dimensions can vary according to individual needs but the overall width must be at least seven feet, preferably nine feet. The stage is made in three sections; the front and two wings. If it is necessary to make the center section in two pieces, join the pieces with 1"x 2" braces on the back. The

paneling should then be securely attached to the PVC pipe frame described above in the one-level curtain stage. The paneling can be attached by drilling holes in the pipe and using bolts and wing nuts. Wooden paneling has matching trim and this molding should be used around the sides and top. This is particularly important where the front and sides are hinged together. This joint must be carefully planned to hide the pipe support behind it. Construction of a second wooden panel stage, larger than the one just described, allows performances on two levels. The second level should be approximately 1½ or 2 feet higher than the first. This setup allows some other advantages mentioned in the description of three-level-tiered curtain stages.

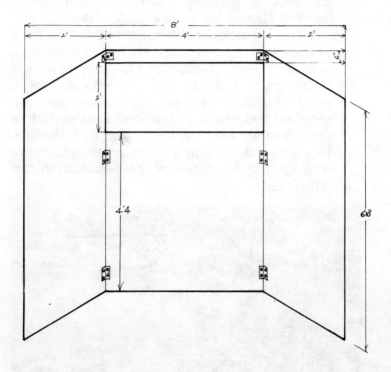

The plywood stage is simple to construct from this diagram and can be decorated according to what is desired by the puppet team. The curtain rod and curtain should be suspended from the back of the wings to form a backdrop for the stage.

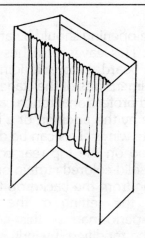

4. A plywood stage can be one of the most attractive and colorful stages available for puppet teams. It is an excellent stage for outdoor performances in parks, shopping center malls, or backyards. This stage can utilize banners, flags, balloons and other festive items to help create a fun, carnival-like atmosphere. The plywood itself can be painted, in solid colors or in designs. This stage is particularly appealing to younger audiences.

  Three sheets of 4x8 plywood are required for this stage. Have one of the sheets cut into two 2x7 sections; these sections will be the stage wings. The remaining sheets will be the center section of the stage. Cut one foot off the top of each sheet. The two 4x7 sections will stand side by side and should be connected with hinges. Permanent brackets are not useful because they add needlessly to the amount of space needed in storage and transportation. With this stage, the puppets appear through an opening, not over the top of the stage. The opening should begin approximately 4 to 4½ feet from the floor, depending on the height of the puppeteers. The opening should be two feet high.

The stage opening should be approximately seven feet wide. This leaves six inches on the side of each plywood board before it joins the side wings. Overall dimensions of the stage opening are 2'x7'. An added professional touch can be achieved with this stage by the addition of a backdrop attached to the side wings. This can be done by attaching a curtain rod on the top rear corner on both side wings. A solid-colored curtain or painted scenery is then hung from the backdrop to help give added flavor to the setting of the puppet play. For outdoor performances this curtain set-up may need to be modified if windy conditions exist. To modify the stage, attach a three foot deep section of ¼ inch plywood where the curtain rod would ordinarily be placed. The plywood should be painted a sky blue and scenery or sets painted on canvas or muslin can then be dropped over the backdrop to achieve the desired scene for the puppet play. These painted scenes will not flap in the breeze because of the wood reinforcing.

5. Other items may also be used as stages to help create special effects. A piano, for example, provides an excellent stage when performing musical numbers, perhaps in tandem with a human pianist. Bookshelves or other items of furniture which block the audience's view of the puppeteer, can also be used. If the production is being taped for television or film, stages need not hide the puppeteers entirely. In such cases, the stage must cover only the section which is actually being recorded by the camera.

Stages are important; they are the first impression which the audience will receive from your puppet team. Even if the puppetry is excellent and all other aspects of the performance go smoothly, a sub-standard stage will detract from the audience's enjoyment of the show. Whichever stage is selected by your puppet group, make sure it is well-constructed and attractive.

A large sheet of corrugated cardboard covered with contact paper makes an excellent stage for the classroom and is easy to put in place. It is not recommended for groups which frequently travel for performances.

19

Props

The use of props lends added realism to any puppet production. The daily activities of human beings are not carried out in an environment devoid of such items as furniture, appliances, decorations, trees, backgrounds, and so on: One of the major failures of amateur puppet shows is the lack of props in their plays. It is impossible to create a realistic western atmosphere, for example, if the puppets perform behind just a simple cloth stage. Puppet teams can paint backgrounds which help the audience visualize a western scene: perhaps a ranch house or corral with mountain backdrop could be used for their play. Background scenes painted on muslin or canvas can also be rolled up and stored for later use. After a brief period of time the puppet team accumulates numerous "sets" — which enable the puppet team to perform almost any production without additional time spent in prop and set construction.

Backgrounds and sets, however, are just one type of prop used in puppet plays. Any item which is easily recognized by the audience and necessary for the play can be used as a prop. The major concern is that the prop be in correct proportion to the puppets themselves. In a play which features a human hand and arm puppet in the role of a football player, for example, a child's football and tiny shoulder pads could be used with excellent results. If the script calls for a woman puppet to rummage through a purse, a small-sized purse would create the best effect. Audiences never fail to respond to musical numbers where the puppets play instruments such as a piano, trumpet, harmonica, etc.

Even rod arm puppets can perform with props such as musical instruments. Attach the prop to the puppet's hand with rubber bands or pipe cleaners.

Although in many instances these instruments require human hand and arm puppets to operate them, there are also musical props for rod arm puppets. Kazoos can be attached to the hand of a rod arm puppet with rubber bands and this unexpected ability delights audiences.

Some props, such as a miniature piano, are not held by the puppet and therefore must be attached in some way so that it may be seen by the audience. The prop rack is built for this purpose. The prop rack is used with the PVC pipe and curtain stage described in the last chapter. Simple to make, the prop rack is made of two 2x2's and four metal "T" brackets. The 2x2's are placed parallel with each other, approximately ¾" apart. (The distance apart is determined by the thickness of the board which will be placed between the 2x2's.) The "T" brackets are then fastened to the boards as shown in the illustration. For added stability, place the brackets on both sides of the 2x2's. To attach the prop rack to the stage, drill a hole through the pipe framework of the stage and insert a bolt and wing nut. This is a sturdy arrangement which is also quick to assemble and disassemble, a consideration important to puppet teams which frequently travel.

This prop rack should be located just beneath the top of the curtain; experiment to see where it should go. If the rack is too low, the audience will have difficulty seeing the prop. To complete the rack, insert a piece of 1x3 snuggly between the crosspieces and put the prop in this "sliding shelf." If the rack is being used in a musical number that requires the puppets to play a piano, drum, etc., you will need to fasten each instrument securely to its own 1x3 shelf.

The prop rack can also be modified slightly and constructed with 1x2's and a U-bolt. The construction of this rack produces exactly the right distance between

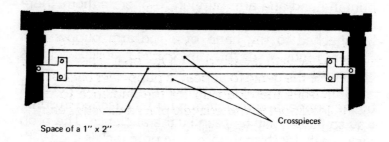

Space of a 1" x 2"   Crosspieces

The prop rack is useful if props must rest on a shelf in view of the audience, during the show. The shelf is inserted in the slot of the prop rack.

crosspieces, since 1x2 spacers are used at intervals across the rack. This rack is also easy to attach to the stage, simply loosening the nuts and sliding the U-bolt down over the pipe supports which form the stage front. As was the case with the first prop rack, 1x3 sliding shelves are inserted between the crosspieces.

If puppets are being used for instructional purposes, props should be constructed which help reinforce the lesson visually. Lessons covering arthmetic or the alphabet, for example, should include either the numbers or letters. To construct these props, simply cut out the desired shape from cardboard and paint it. Then attach the prop to the rods which are used to manipulate rod arm puppets. A puppeteer can then create a "character" from the prop and it can even be shown in speaking parts and pre-recorded tapes by animating the prop. Other cardboard items such as rocks, trees, airplanes, etc., can also be attached to rods and used in this fashion.

Props can also be used to create special effects. In a story about Aladdin's lamp, the genie appears in a make-believe puff of smoke. Props are used to accomplish this. A cloud is shaped out of cardboard and painted white with the word "POOF" on it. Then, when it is time for the genie to appear, a puppeteer backstage quickly pushes the cloud up for the audience to see. The genie puppet is immediately placed directly behind this cloud and becomes visible to the audience as the cloud is lowered.

Props are not absolutely essential for the production of a puppet show, but they do add credibility to the performance. The puppet team which shows pride in its accomplishments and is constantly striving for excellence will want to utilize props to the maximum advantage. Like the icing on a cake, it makes a good thing even better.

Painted backdrops help create the mood of the play. This marionette show looks like it is being performed inside a old-fashioned home.

20

Costumes

If the clothes help make the man, then the costumes certainly help the puppet. Creative costumes will greatly enhance the ability of your puppets to perform in a wide variety of roles. Costumes help create the mood being set; they add to the believability of the character. Most puppets are received in an average-looking shirt or blouse, but these costumes should certainly not be the entire wardrobe of *your* puppets.

Patterns are available for sewing various costumes or toddler size 2 clothing from the store fits most rod arm puppets perfectly. Do you have a cowboy character in your play? How about a bandana neckerchief and a boy's hat? Hats remain in place better if they are pinned on. Several long straight pins are sufficient to do this. Overalls and dungaree material can be used for a wide variety of characters, including a train conductor and farmer. Sports personalities are easy to portray merely by suggesting the particular sport with its uniform: a baseball cap, basketball shirt or football shoulder pads. Dress your boxer in a bath robe or the starlet behind "Elton John" sunglasses. The only consideration in costuming is that the dress be consistent with the character.

A church, for example, should not use a shabbily-dressed puppet to represent a rich tax collector. Puppet shows must be believable, and costuming is a significant part of this believability. If schools are relating the ethnic backgrounds of minority groups, they may wish to costume puppets in dress which has been associated with them traditionally. The puppet director must exercise judgment in this case to insure that stereotypes are not being taught, but this can be done and still have the puppet wear native dress.

Costumes are excellent ways of giving the historical setting of the puppet show. Puppets should accurately reflect the dress of the time period in their play. Biblical figures would be dressed in robes; a suit of armor could be constructed of cardboard or maybe aluminum foil for a Saxon knight.

As you are by now aware, costuming is limited only by the imagination of the director or individual puppeteer. How would you dress a French Legionnaire? Pancho Villa? Ferdinand Magellen? Abraham Lincoln? It is not too difficult to sew a powdered wig for George Washington. The possibilities are endless.

Minor costume changes can radically change the personality. A boy puppet becomes a girl with the addition of a head scarf and necklace. And the addition of a colorful floppy hat transforms an Afro boy into a woman.

One of the goals of an experienced puppeteer is to create a personality in his puppet, to make it believable, even human. Clothing, jewelry, wigs, and other costuming items are an excellent way to create this realistic effect.

21

Sound System And Microphones

One of the main failures of many puppet groups is their attempt to perform without an adequate sound system. Puppets, whether acting as entertainers or teachers, must be understandable if they are to be successful in holding the attention of an audience. Puppet teams which do not devote enough attention to their sound system will not be successful, regardless of how accomplished they may be in the art of puppetry.

An adequate system need not be an expensive one, but it must be able to amplify both the puppeteers' voices and pre-recorded tapes. A medium-size guitar amp-speaker is sufficient for audiences of less than 100. This amplifier must have at least three inputs; these inputs can be expanded by using "Y" adaptors and plugging two microphones into one input.

For audiences numbering more than 100, larger systems are required. Some puppet teams invest in

The headset microphone is best suited for puppet shows since the microphone remains a constant distance from the puppeteer's mouth, regardless of the action performed.

their own portable systems which best fit their needs. Other teams often make use of existing systems in the buildings where they perform, such as the "house system" in a church or school auditorium. Sound systems must be carefully treated and thoroughly checked out before each performance. It is embarrassing and unprofessional to have to stop a performance in order to correct minor malfunctions. And the alternative, continuing the show with improper sound, is equally unthinkable. The puppet director or sound man should insure that all components are in proper working order before the show begins. Unlike the use of lights or props, sound systems are not optional; they are a must for every quality puppet team.

All puppet teams will perform pre-recorded programs. Accordingly, a tape recorder must be listed in the inventory of items in the sound system. The recorder may be either cassette or reel-to-reel, although cassettes have been found to be faster and easier to use.

Another vital part of any sound system is the microphone. Microphones are necessary when any part of the performance is "live." Puppeteer voices must be amplified if they are to be heard and understood. Many puppet teams are affiliated with institutions which already own microphones of some type, institutions such as churches or schools. Other groups, even the more ambitious church and school teams, will want to purchase microphones exclusively for puppet team use.

Four different types of microphone arrangements have been found to be satisfactory for use with puppet teams.

1.   HEADSET — (Electro-Voice Model RE51 Miniature Dynamic).

This is the best microphone arrangement for puppeteers. The head microphone always remains

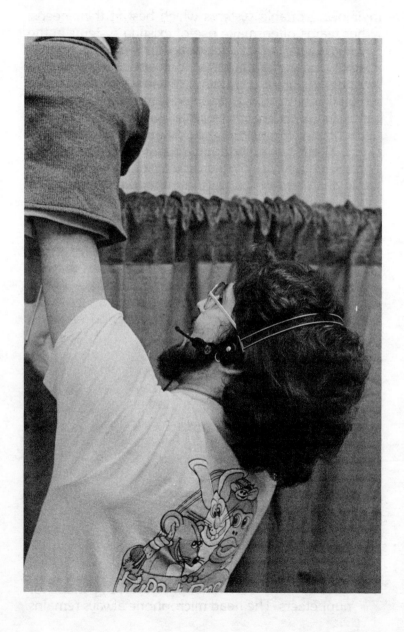

the same distance from the speaker's mouth, providing constant sound levels. The RE51 is designed for professional use in broadcasting, performing, lecturing, etc., when hand-free operation is a major consideration. It is a low impedance microphone but can be converted to use with a high impedance amplifier by No. A95P Line Matching Transformer by Shure.

2. STANDS — This arrangement is a simple microphone on a microphone stand. It can be used adequately by one or two persons, as long as the puppeteers remember to speak directly into the microphone. Most churches or schools already have this system and it can be utilized by the puppet team.

3. CRADLE — The cradle microphone is a regular microphone attached to a metal necklace. This system cannot be purchased but must be specially constructed by a blacksmith. He should form the metal rod to fit around the puppeteer's neck, with the microphone cradle attached.

4. LAPEL — A lavaliere is a lapel microphone. There are several companies making this type of microphone. Shure has three or four models of lavaliere microphones which fit around your neck; their prices vary considerably and you will want to shop for the best bargain on this item.

Sound systems are one of the most important aspects of a quality puppet production. There is a wide range of systems available and the cost involved is also quite wide-ranging, depending on the system selected. Puppet teams may use any system they wish, the only common denominator which links all systems is this: they must be capable of producing a sound good enough to attract the audience.

A regular microphone attached to a mike stand is used by this puppeteer to perform a live show.

22

Lighting

Many puppet teams are content to operate with only the minimum equipment necessary: puppets, stage, and sound system. But the puppet team which wants quality will want to invest a few dollars more to operate an inexpensive lighting system. This will greatly help your puppet productions have a professional flavor, and the added cost is minor.

There are several methods of creating an inexpensive portable lighting system. For more permanent theatres or studios, a lighting consultant may be necessary to customize the system for the building.

The least expensive and most portable set-up utilizes three microphone stands as "trees" or light stands. The conversion of the stands to light structures involves attaching a 150 watt spotlight to the top of each tree. The spotlight should be encased in an aluminum cylinder (three pound coffee cans will suffice) or spotlamp holder. In this arrangement one of the lamps should be white and the other two should be pink, or if available, amber.

The white spot should be positioned approximately four to six feet in front of center stage and should shine upward from below stage level. If the stage front is four feet high, the light should be approximately two to three feet off the floor. The two pink or amber lamps must be stationed to either side of the stage, approximately two to three feet from the stage itself, and directly in line with each other and the stage front. The lights should be focused on center stage and should shine down from their elevated position, 4½ to 5 feet from the floor.

This illustration shows how lights and sound should be positioned in relationship to the stage. Side lights beam down from above stage level and the center light is aimed upward.

This small lighting system is excellent for puppet teams which are just getting established. It is designed to be used in conjunction with the regular overhead lighting of smaller buildings. If the play is being performed before larger audiences, or without added lights, lamps with additional wattage will be necessary. This is an excellent and inexpensive way to adequately light your puppet stage.

As needs and experience dictate, a more powerful system may be desired. This can be done without sacrificing the portability of professional theatre lights. The lamps and fixtures in this system are marketed under the name "Power-Trac" by Halo, a trademark of the Mc Graw-Edison Company. The lamps themselves come in 200 watts (L431) and 300 watts. Experience has shown that white lamps are best in the center of the stage with pink or amber well-suited for both wings. The lamps should be placed atop microphone stands or light trees and positioned further from the stage than in the less expensive system described before. With the more powerful lights, it may be necessary to station the side lamp even higher, to eliminate shadows. If a boom mike stand is used, the side lamps can be as high as seven feet.

This system can become a permanent one by installing a trac or bar receptacle in the ceiling. For a portable system adapt the fixtures in the following way:
1. Cut the exposed wire at the back of the fixture and splice it to an extension a/c cord.
2. Remove the trac adapter from the frame.
3. Bolt the fixture on a light tree or stand.
4. If microphone stands are being used instead of light trees, purchase mike stand adaptors that screw into the top of the stand. They can be permanently attached to the light fixture by drilling two holes into the adjustable black frame and

bolting the mike stand adaptor to the light fixture. Individual puppet teams may desire more lamps, especially if the system is to be a permanent one and if the building is large. But the basic requirements of lighting for puppet productions can be met with three lamps and the system is easily transported and assembled. Whichever method the individual puppet team selects should be based on their particular needs.

23

Special Effects

The use of special effects adds a delightful dimension to quality puppet performances. But special effects should not be attempted until; the puppet team is thoroughly familiar with all the aspects of puppetry. Puppeteers must be accomplished, and the entire team should have a complete repertoire of plays for audiences of differing orientation. Once a puppet team reaches this level of expertise, however, they will want to perform with special effects to further enhance their productions. A few ideas for special-effect puppetry are listed here. Experience and creative minds will generate additional ones.

1. WHITE GLOVES. This technique utilizes just a puppeteer and a pair of white gloves. It is performed under black light. The puppeteer is clothed completely in black and, under the light, becomes invisible to the audience. The white gloves

These drawings show how the puppeteer positions himself behind the human-sized puppets for performances with black light. When the black light is on, only the colorful, fluorescent puppet is seen.

themselves become the puppets. This is an excellent technique for performing musical numbers. One or more pairs of gloves may be used and the creative person will choreograph the white gloves into an extremely entertaining number.

The white gloves technique can also be used for instructional purposes. The hands can perform various tasks, with the children being asked to determine what the hands are doing. For example, a music class could benefit from guessing what type of instrument is being played just from the hand gestures. Trombones would have one hand stationary with the other sliding in front of it; flutes would have active finger movement and the hands side by side. The possibilities are endless. This is an excellent method for visual learning, one which would be particularly effective for those who do not respond well to traditional auditory experiences.

2. FLUORESCENT PUPPETS. This is another entertaining special effect which utilizes black light and special puppets with fluorescent materials. In this, as in the white glove technique, a 100-watt mercury arc, high intensity flood lamp should be approximately 4-6 feet in front of the stage and at ceiling height. Puppets should be dressed in costumes of fluorescent fabric. Any props such as backdrops, hats, gloves, musical instruments, umbrellas, etc., should be spray-painted with fluorescent paint. When only the black light is on to illuminate this scene, the resultant colorful performance is hard to imagine. Once again, only the limits of your imagination restrict the use of black lights and fluorescent colors. With this technique, a quality puppet show becomes even more stimulating.

An educational use of this technique involves a special human hand and arm puppet, with fluorescent costume and white gloves. This puppet can use a chalkboard and fluorescent chalk to illuminate the lesson; good method of dual-mode instruction.

3.   HUMAN-SIZED PUPPETS. This special effect also utilizes black lights which are positioned the same as above. In this technique, the puppeteer actually becomes the arms and legs of the puppet. A specially-constructed puppet is also required.

This technique is a new innovation in creative puppetry. A special set is needed to create the desired effect. The set, or stage, consists of a 12-foot wide black curtain, that hangs from ceiling to floor. In front of the curtain, place three sheets of 4x8 plywood that have been painted with flat black paint. This gives a floor performing area eight feet deep and twelve feet wide. The black floor must meet the black curtain. If sheets of black vinyl flooring are available, they would be excellent for the flooring, and they provide portability not available with the plywood sheets.

The black stage is now set for the puppet and puppeteer. A special puppet is necessary for this effect. [These puppets are available from Puppet Productions in San Diego, California.] Unlike other hand-held puppets, this puppet has a complete, human-sized body, including legs. The puppeteer inserts one hand into the head to manipulate the mouth and the other hand is inserted into one arm. The puppet is especially constructed with a dummy arm. The body and legs of the puppet are attached to the puppet with straps.

The puppeteer must be dressed completely in black to keep from being seen. This includes slippers and a black mask to cover the face and head (a ski mask is ideal). This technique is very difficult to master because it involves extreme coordination to present the desired effect. Movements are restricted by the need to maintain the puppet in absolute alignment, directly in front of the puppeteer. The purpose of this innovative technique is to present a human-like performance from head to toe. The puppet head is similar to the regular puppet and allows realistic lip sync to either dialog or music numbers. This is especially appealing with a fully-choreographed production. The twelve-foot-wide stage is enough room for three or four such "puppets."

Special effects are just that: they are special. They should be attempted only to complement a basic puppet performance. These techniques require a mastery of the fundamentals of puppetry. In the hands of experienced puppeteers, they are highly entertaining. Beginning puppeteers should master the basics before they attempt to utilize special effects in their performances!

24

Puppetry On Wheels

Energetic puppet teams do not have to wait for audiences to come to them. They will take their shows to shopping centers, malls, parks, wherever people gather. For these groups, mobile puppet stages are extremely useful.

Mobile puppet stages come in all shapes and sizes. Vans or trucks can be converted for temporary use as stages. Simply drive up, open the doors, turn on the sound, and begin! A tension bar is used to hang a curtain across the door opening. The puppeteers either sit or kneel inside the van to perform.

A similar stage can be constructed out of enclosed U-Haul type trailers. The stage opening can be either the double doors in the rear of the trailer or a special opening cut out of the side. Either way, care should be taken.to insure that the stage is visually pleasing since this will definitely affect the first impression of the

This bus, Mr. Quimper's Good Time Show, has been completely converted to a mobile puppet stage. The outside has been decorated with puppets to attract the attention of children when the bus travels to perform in shopping centers, parks, or neighborhoods.

audience and will play a large role in their enjoyment of the show. Vans and trailers both require a power source to run the necessary sound systems.

More ambitious puppet teams may be interested in converting an old bus into a mobile puppet stage. This has been done with spectacular results. The first order of business is to obtain the bus. This is a relatively simple task since many old buses are surplus because they are no longer in good enough working order to carry passengers. The interior of the bus should be completely stripped and a stage constructed at the rear of the bus. Allow enough room behind the stage for puppet storage, sound system and lighting controls. A basic system of spot lights should be installed in the ceiling as described in chapter 25. The sound system should be adequate for the interior acoustics of the bus.

The audience can sit on the floor after it has been carpeted. Extending the carpet up the walls and even on the ceiling enhances the interior and also serves to insulate the bus from outside sounds. The windows will have to be covered, serving the dual purpose of darkening the stage and cutting off distractions from the outside.

Inside Mr. Quimper's Good Time Show is a complete stage built into the back of the bus. The passenger compartment is carpeted floor to ceiling and children sit on the floor to watch the show.

A main advantage of the bus stage is the ability of adult puppet team sponsors to control the behavior of the audience. Crowds which stand and watch a show from the sidewalk may become loud or unruly and the puppet team is powerless to influence this behavior. It is not the same situation with an audience that views a puppet show from *inside* the mobile stage. In this instance, those who might become disruptive can be asked to leave and the show can continue. Also, having the audience enter the bus often serves to discourage disruptive behavior, since the circumstances are similar to visting the house of a stranger: good manners are generally much in evidence.

Mobile puppet stages allow performances anywhere. It is not important whether your team is capable of operating an expensive and sophisticated mobile stage. What is important is the willingness to perform "where the people are" and the ability to construct a mobile stage that is sufficient for the task.

NOTES

NOTES